This memoir is dedicated to my father, Van Wolf Kogul, whose heroic survival is documented in the pages that follow. This book equally serves to honor those who survived, as well as those who perished, in WWII and the Holocaust in the Allied fight against the Nazis. May their memories serve as an eternal reminder to "Never Forget," and stand against tyranny of all forms.

www.mascotbooks.com

Running Breathless: An Untold True Story of WWII and The Holocaust

For more information, please contact:
Mascot Books
620 Herndon Parkway, Suite 320
Herndon, VA 20170
info@mascotbooks.com

Library of Congress Control Number: 2018900047

CPSIA Code: PROPM0918B
ISBN-13: 978-1-68401-732-4

Printed in the United States

RUNNING BREATHLESS

An Untold True Story of WWII and the Holocaust

By Morey Kogul

Contents

Introduction

In September 1939, just prior to the outbreak of World War II, Germany and the Soviet Union implemented the Molotov–Ribbentrop Pact—dividing Poland between the two nations and erasing it from the map. On September 18, 1939, Soviet forces occupied the Polish city of Dubno and proceeded to eradicate nearly all traces of public Jewish life. The Soviets liquidated Jewish community institutions, banned all political parties, and transferred Jewish welfare services to the municipality. All Jewish economic enterprises and buildings were nationalized, and Jewish leaders were arrested. For nearly two years, the Jews of Dubno would live hidden and persecuted lives under Soviet control.

On June 22, 1941, Germany launched Operation Barbarossa—a massive, surprise invasion of the Soviet Union—in flagrant disregard of Molotov-Ribbentrop's guarantees of mutual non-aggression. By June 25, the German army had entered Dubno, leaving the local population with little to no time to escape.

In connivance with the German invaders, the local Ukrainian population unleashed a violent pogrom against Dubno's Jews, wantonly robbing, maiming, and murdering. The Germans themselves, meanwhile, confiscated money and valuables from the Jewish community. On July 22, 1941, 80 Jews were executed by the Nazis in the local cemetery. One month later, 900 more were killed. The Germans organized a local Jewish administrative council, or *Judenrat*, to enforce Nazi control and conscripted the Jewish population into forced labor. The winter that followed was marked by disease and hunger. Despite attempts to provide relief by self-organizing Jewish public kitchens, many in the community succumbed to the unbearable conditions.

In early April 1942, the Germans sorted the Jewish population into two ghettoes, one for workers and their families and the second for the rest.

Over the course of two days, beginning on May 26, 1942, the Germans murdered all the Jews in the second ghetto, burying them in mass graves on the outskirts of the city. In August 1942, Jews from outlying regions and other survivors were rounded up and relocated to the first ghetto. Over the first week of October, 1942, about 4,500 inhabitants of the ghetto were murdered. Another 353 Jews, needed artisans who'd been briefly reprieved, were murdered on October 23. Fourteen Jews managed to escape.

During the war crimes trial at Nuremberg following the war, German construction engineer Hermann Friedrich Graebe provided an eyewitness account of the October 5 atrocities:

> From September 1941 to January 1944 I was director and chief engineer of the Zdolbunow branch of the Josef Jung Construction Company of Solingen. In this capacity I had, among my other duties, to visit the firm's projects. Under the terms of a contract with the army construction services, the company was to build grain warehouses on the old Dubno airfield in the Ukraine.
>
> On October 5, 1942, at the time of my visit to the construction offices in Dubno, my foreman, Hubert Moennikes, living at 21 Aussenmühlenweg, Hamburg-Haarburg, told me that some Dubno Jews had been shot near the building in three huge ditches about 30 meters long and 3 meters deep. The number of people killed daily was about 1,500. The 5,000 Jews who had lived in Dubno before the Pogrom were all marked for liquidation. Since the executions took place in the presence of my employee, he was painfully impressed by them.
>
> Accompanied by Moennikes, I then went to the work area. I saw great mounds of earth about 30 meters long and 2 high. Several trucks were parked nearby. Armed Ukrainian militia were making people get out, under the surveillance

of SS soldiers. The same militiamen were responsible for guard duty and driving the trucks. The people in the trucks wore the regulation yellow pieces of cloth that identified them as Jews on the front and back of their clothing.

Moennikes and I went straight toward the ditches without being stopped. When we neared the mound, I heard a series of rifle shots close by. The people from the trucks – men, women and children – were forced to undress under the supervision of an SS soldier with a whip in his hand. They were obliged to put their effects in certain spots: shoes, clothing, and underwear separately. I saw a pile of shoes, about 800-1,000 pairs, great heaps of underwear and clothing. Without weeping or crying out, these people undressed and stood together in family groups, embracing each other and saying goodbye while waiting for a sign from the SS soldier, who stood on the edge of the ditch, a whip in his hand, too. During the fifteen minutes I stayed there, I did not hear a single complaint, or plea for mercy. I watched a family of about eight: a man and woman about fifty years old, surrounded by their children of about one, eight, and ten, and two big girls about twenty and twenty-four. An old lady, her hair completely white, held the baby in her arms, rocking it, and singing it a song. The infant was crying aloud with delight. The parents watched the groups with tears in their eyes. The father held the ten-year-old boy by the hand, speaking softly to him: The child struggled to hold back his tears. Then the father pointed a finger to the sky, and, stroking the child's head, seemed to be explaining something. At this moment, the SS near the ditch called something to his comrade. The latter counted off some twenty people and ordered them behind the mound. The family of which I have just spoken was in the group.

I still remember the young girl, slender and dark, who, passing near me, pointed at herself, saying, "twenty-three." I walked around the mound and faced a frightful common grave. Tightly packed corpses were heaped so close together that only the heads showed. Most were wounded in the head and the blood flowed over their shoulders. Some still moved. Others raised their hands and turned their heads to show that they were still alive. The ditch was two-thirds full. I estimate that it held a thousand bodies. I turned my eyes toward the man who had carried out the execution. He was an SS man; he was seated, legs swinging, on the narrow edge of the ditch; an automatic rifle rested on his knees and he was smoking a cigarette. The people, completely naked, climbed down a few steps cut in the clay wall and stopped at the spot indicated by the SS man. Facing the dead and wounded, they spoke softly to them. Then I heard a series of rifle shots. I looked in the ditch and saw their bodies contorting, their heads, already inert, sinking on the corpses beneath. The blood flowed from the nape of their necks. I was astonished not to be ordered away, but I noticed two or three uniformed postmen nearby. A new batch of victims approached the place. They climbed down into the ditch, lined up in front of the previous victims, and were shot.

On the way back, while rounding the mound, I saw another full truck, which had just arrived. This truck contained only the sick and crippled. Women already naked were undressing an old woman with an emaciated body; her legs frightfully thin. She was held up by two people and seemed paralyzed. The naked people led her behind the mound. I left the place with Moennikes and went back to Dubno in a car.

The next morning, returning to the construction, I saw some thirty naked bodies lying thirty to fifty yards from the ditch. Some were still alive; they stared into space with a set look, seeming not to feel the coolness of the morning air; nor to see the workers standing around. A young girl of about twenty spoke to me, asking me to bring her clothes and to help her escape. At that moment we heard the sound of a car approaching at top speed; I saw that it was an SS detachment. I went back to my work. Ten minutes later rifle shots sounded from the ditch The Jews who were still alive had been ordered to throw the bodies in the ditch; then they had to lie down themselves to receive a bullet in the back of the neck.[i]

By the time the war was over, only about 300 Jews from Dubno remained alive. Among them was a small group of young Jewish men who fled the German invasion of eastern Poland in 1941 and managed to escape into the sprawling interior of the Soviet Union. My father was one of them. This is his story.

Prologue

The Battle of Budapest was upon us. We all knew it. Each day was long and exhausting, and now it was getting darker, colder. The casualties would be severe, as always. News from the front showed signs of hope, but in the midst of these losses, the countless dead, it was difficult to see victory.

"Vladimir Nusseyonovich!" called my superior officer. I hastily ran over to review the communications plans under a drenched and tattered tarp. The makeshift field command post was a dank space filled with maps, cigarette smoke, and sooty tables. The accumulated stress of three years of war creased the officers' faces. We were all in a continuous, evolving state of grief, mourning the living as much as the dead. Huddled around battle maps covered with lines, arrows, and operational symbols, we received our orders. Strategies in place, we all knew our roles. A quick salute concluded the meeting, and we filed out slowly to receive our rations.

With my tin of boiled potato soup, a Soviet army staple, I sat on an embankment on the east side of the Danube, overlooking the city. I pulled out my weathered wooden spoon from my three-year-old leather boots and peered across the river through the thick, low fog that shrouded the city skyline on the opposite bank. The steel-gray river, winding slowly under its historic bridges and around the far shore, appeared ominous and imposing. Lost in the movement of water, I was swallowed by my memories. Faces of my lost friends. The embrace of my family. My stolen home. Yiddish jokes, Polish insults, Russian orders, German threats...all swirling in my mind.

The hum of an airplane motor, high above the clouds, rattled me from my thoughts. Noticing my cooling soup and the pang of hunger from my stomach, I dipped the spoon into the hearty broth, careful not to spill any of the precious liquid. The aircraft engines vibrated and buzzed louder. It was just as I placed the spoon into my mouth that the silhouette emerged. Then one lone, streaking sound split the sky. A rhythmic procession of whistles followed. Air raid alarms reverberated across the river banks. I gasped in sudden terror, choking on the soup, transfixed by the falling bomb. At any moment there would be a deafening crash, debris flung in all directions, panic and chaos. Time and space stood still, save for that never-ending whistle.

I coughed incessantly to clear my lungs, willing myself to break free from my paralyzed state. Scrambling to my feet, the tin of soup tumbled off my knee into the river below; yet another meal stolen by this war. Racing for safety from the impending doom, a surprising feeling came over me: I suddenly realized that I actually cared whether or not I lived or died. Up until this point, I had been resigned to whatever miserable fate this savage war held in store for me. Now, after three years of hell, I vowed to myself: *I am going to survive.*

PART 1 – REFUGEE

Chapter 1:
Passover

I couldn't fully appreciate the foreboding that enveloped my father during our final Passover meal together. I wish I could tell you my father was wrong. I wish it all would have come out differently. That is the hard part: living with loss...and the guilt of surviving.

You see, at the time, life for me was a game. No matter how dire the circumstances, I couldn't be bothered with worry. Perhaps I was oblivious. *Wolf-a-Blinder*. That's me. Literally, *blinder* means blind. But as is so common in Yiddish, the literal is only skin deep. We never used proper names. Only nicknames. I was blind to the consequences of my actions, hence, the affectionate *Wolf-a-Blinder*.

He was an imposing figure, my father. He was tall, muscular, and had a full head of thick hair. He was also charming, witty, and a successful businessman. At least that's how I'd always pictured him.

It was Passover during spring, 1941, when I sat next to him, studying the distant look in his eyes. I couldn't reconcile my mental image of my father with the hollowed man sitting at the head of our Passover table. Two years of stress, anxiety, and scarcity had taken a severe toll. His hair had grayed and thinned; his crisp, custom-tailored clothes hung off of him loosely. He looked much like every other father in Dubno, desperately planning, hoping to keep his family safe. The most striking change to me was the absent stare; the look of invincibility in his eyes was gone. But he put on a brave face, every day. And despite the degrading conditions in our world, he insisted we continue to practice and honor our traditions—and hold a Passover Seder, just as our ancestors did for thousands of years before.

As the twilight sky showcased the first evening stars, we began to settle in around the Passover table. Our Seder this year seemed smaller and more subdued compared with the lively crowds that filled our home for Jewish holidays in years past. Still, we were lucky to have each other—something my mother would remind us of daily. We each took turns washing our hands according to custom, and in silent prayer I returned to the table. Squeezing between the wall and dining room chairs, I found myself facing the portrait of Sholem Aleichem hanging in our front hall. Looking at the picture, I drifted off in memories, recalling the Jewish community of my youth in Dubno, before Poland was torn in half.

✡

August, 1939, changed everything for us. Before that, there was life—childhood, weddings, dreams, and plans. After, there was unending nervous fear. For nearly 300 years, Dubno had been home to Jews, who had grown to a vibrant community of approximately 15,000 by the time I was born in 1922. My father, Nussen Kogul, was a successful fabrics merchant. He married my mother, Chana Grossberg, and had three children—my older sister, Sarah, younger brother Moshe, and me, Yonah Wolf. My brother and sister were model children: they were respectful, courteous, and dutiful. You could say that I was the black sheep.

If there was mischief to be made, I would find it. At 10 years old, I climbed a two-story electric pole in the town center to the cheers and jeers of my classmates. I whooped and hollered from the top, staring at a potentially perilous fall with a defiant smile. My poor mother. When she arrived pale and frightened, she gently called for me to come down, praying I wouldn't slip. When I finally reached the ground, she dragged me by my ear all the way home and walloped my rear so hard it hurt to sit for two days—all because she loved me so much.

Then there was the time I took my father's brand new leather boots to a cobbler because I wanted a soccer ball. The cobbler protested, but I convinced him that my father didn't object. I came home that evening beaming in quiet pride: My father's boots had been trimmed into a pair of loafers—and I had a perfect soccer ball! Brazenly, I placed the shoes and the ball next to one another in our coat closet. The next morning when my father went for his shoes, he shouted an awful thunder of curses and promptly applied the loafer repeatedly to my backside.

Of course, my favorite act of rebellion will have to be blamed simply on teenage hormones. Sarah was an aspiring seamstress and had a talent for sewing women's undergarments. When her clients would come to our house to try on her wares, she directed them to a makeshift fitting room. I found a hole in the wall that provided just the right amount of visibility to peer discreetly into Sarah's fitting room. I'd invite my friends over to see the show, and we would laugh in hysterics. This lasted a good while, until my mother walked in and caught the side of my face plastered to the wall, mesmerized by naked curves. Jovially aghast, she slapped me sternly on the backside for my behavior. As I jumped, startled and blushing with shame, she laughed.

Hotheaded, I found myself in frequent fistfights with Polish kids that spat anti-Semitic slurs at us. And heaven help us when our Jewish soccer team would defeat the local Polish squad. Pandemonium. Every kid came home with a bloodied shirt and black eye. And how can I forget Sundays? Following church sermons, which always seemed to vilify Jews for the ills of Europe, Polish youth attacked their Jewish neighbors on the street and vandalized and destroyed Jewish establishments.

Despite our hardships, life was pretty good. We had a wonderful synagogue led by spiritual rabbis and a great community club that organized cultural, athletic, and political events. I have many wonderful memories of my childhood. I participated in Maccabi soccer and boxing programs, played second baritone in the local band, and attended nearly every dance and social event organized by our community to celebrate rich Jewish traditions. Being the object of hatred was a painful fact of life that Jews endured for thousands of years, but somehow we managed to live a relatively peaceful life in Poland—until Poland vanished from the map.

As the autumn leaves began to change in 1939, the secret protocol of the Molotov–Ribbentrop Pact was implemented. Germany and the Soviet Union drew a line down the center of Poland and divided our country. Every soul in Dubno was shaken to the core, so frightened that denial offered the only emotional relief. In the immediate days following the announcement, the Jewish club of Dubno became a daily gathering point for news and information. Meetings were tense and often chaotic—people talking over one another, expressing opinions ranging from fear to optimism. The anti-Semitic rhetoric coming from the West in Germany, Soviet pogroms to the East, and hostility from neighboring Poles left many of us feeling isolated from the rest of the world, surrounded by enemies. Given the rumors and reports of Nazi persecution against German Jews, many Jews felt that it would be safer to be on the Russian side.

Stanislaw, a bookish but respected Pole who worked as a clerk in the Dubno City Hall, came to speak to the Jewish community about the possible implications of the division of Poland. Stanislaw said that Dubno, with an airport, would become a strategic hub for Soviet military operations, drawing a steady stream of military and government officials. The most significant impact would likely be imposition of communist rule. Stanislaw explained that, under communism, there would no longer be any Jewish-owned businesses or activities. Our despair was alleviated only by our relief that at least we hadn't fallen into German hands.

Stanislaw developed personal relationships with members of the Jewish business community, including my father. As tensions continued to rise in Dubno, Stanislaw was instrumental in facilitating now-prohibited commerce between Jewish merchants and non-Jewish businessmen outside Dubno. I'd always liked Stanislaw. He seemed like a virtuous person. Later, when I needed his help most, I would receive it. But I'll get to that in a while.

During those years before the outbreak of war on the Eastern Front, there was a palpable tension in the rooms of the Jewish Community Center when political issues were discussed; and, at that time, everything was political. Many sensed and feared impending war. Among the Poles, there was nationalistic anger, coupled with the usual anti-Semitism. In 1938, Germany instructed the Czechs to invade Poland in order to gain control of its precious coal mines. The Poles turned to the Polish Jews for help, beseeching them to take up arms and fight the invading Czechs and Germans. Coming from the same people who assaulted us and vandalized our businesses, the request fell on deaf ears; we refused to engage in any conflict. This, of course, further fueled Polish hatred of their Jewish compatriots.

On September 18, 1939, Dubno was occupied by Soviet forces. The Soviet authorities liquidated Jewish community institutions, outlawed all political parties, and transferred Jewish welfare institutions to the municipality. Only one Jewish activity was allowed—the public kitchen for refugees from the West. Jewish leaders, including David Perl, president of the Zionist Organization, were arrested.[ii] All Jewish economic enterprises and buildings were nationalized. Overnight, free market enterprises were illegal, and my father's business closed. Scholars, merchants, tradesmen—all were forced to work Soviet state jobs while trading goods on the black market to provide necessities for their families.

The autumn and winter of 1939 were full of tension. My father no longer received new materials and supplies, leaving him to plan for an uncertain future without knowing how long his inventory would last. Increasingly, food was rationed, forcing us into difficult choices between the risks of illegal black-market deals or facing short-term hunger and threats to our long-term survival.

As the seasons passed, every household in Dubno crafted secret plans and contingencies in the event war broke out. Being a naturally charismatic merchant, my father had numerous business partners with whom he maintained contact under communism, working discreetly through Stanislaw and the black market to meet the continuing demand for clothing. One such contact, a Ukrainian named Mudrik, had a daughter Sarah's age who, like Sarah, was an aspiring seamstress. My father developed a close business relationship with Mudrik, and they considered one another friends, bonding over shared business and family values. With war ever threatening, my father arranged a meeting with Mudrik to discuss a grave request.

Mudrik visited our house late one night. They argued for nearly an hour. I could hardly make out their whispers. Fearful for Sarah's safety, my father beseeched Mudrik to take her in and protect her in the event war broke out. Mudrik said he was sympathetic to my father's plea, but worried about the safety of his own family. My father offered Mudrik a large share of his textiles and leather goods as a sign of appreciation and to compensate Mudrik for the risk. At first, Mudrik refused. My father insisted. Back and forth they went, agonizing over the fate of their children. In the end, Mudrik concluded that since Sarah—a tall, beautiful, blue-eyed, blonde-haired woman—did not display stereotypically Jewish dark hair and dark eyes, he would be able to confidently conceal her identity. My father prepared a bundle of textiles for Mudrik to take home with him. Holding the precious materials, Mudrik consented to my father's request while expressing the hope that it would never become necessary to fulfill it. They agreed that if war broke out, my father would escort Sarah personally to Mudrik's home along with a cartload of fabric and textiles.

I didn't know Mudrik well, only speaking with him briefly when he met with my father during the years of peace. After that night, I would never see him again—which was lucky for him, given what I might have done had I ever found him...but I'll get to that later.

I remember one day in early spring of 1941, Sarah came into the house pale as a ghost and shaking, with Moshe trying to console her. My father held her and eased her to the living room sofa. We gathered around her to hear what had so distressed her.

"Mudrik's daughter, Natasha, and I were working together in Mudrik's shop, like we do every day," Sarah began slowly. "Natasha has a boyfriend—I'm not supposed to tell anyone—a Ukrainian soldier that she met not long ago. She sneaks away during the day to meet with him, and leaves me to do her work, but I don't complain to Mudrik because I don't want to come between you, Papa, and your relationship with him."

Still trembling and racing through her words, Sarah took a deep breath to calm herself. "So when she came back from her latest tryst," she continued, "I told her she wouldn't get any better without the practice, and it wasn't fair for her to leave me with all of her work; I needed her help to finish the orders."

Sarah looked at us for sympathy. "I wasn't trying to be mean to her," she said. "I just didn't want us to get in trouble."

Sarah dabbed her eyes. "Then," she resumed, "Natasha glared at me and said, 'You should feel lucky to have this job. Pretty soon you'll be lucky to be alive.'

"I shook and asked her what she was talking about. How could she speak to me this way after all the years we've known each other?

"Natasha flipped her hair and said, 'My boyfriend told me that they were going to kill all of the Jews in Wolyn, but you are lucky because my father agreed to protect you because your father paid him with all your belongings—typical Jew.'

"I froze. What could I say to that? Natasha saw the fear in my eyes. She smiled. 'Oh, I wouldn't worry; your papa took care of you,' she said. And then she walked out, just like that."

My mother held Sarah and looked at my father. My father patted Sarah on the knee, stood and rubbed his chin as he considered the situation. "Mudrik has been a loyal business partner," he said. "I know his daughter is a little wild, but let's not worry too much. I'm sure Mudrik will do everything to protect you, G-d forbid a war breaks out. Just keep focused on your work, and don't bring up any more arguments with Natasha."

My mother took Sarah off to lie down, and Moshe and I sat in the living room, staring absently, reflecting on what our sister had said. My mother soon returned, and with a confident air, she assured us that everything would be alright. Changing the subject, she asked Moshe and me to go and pick up flour from the market so that she could prepare a challah for the Shabbat meal.

On our walk, Moshe was in deep despair. "Do you think it's true...kill all the Jews?" he mumbled. I shrugged and tried to downplay the frightening message as one of many threats against Jews in our region. But Moshe was always more perceptive and mature than I. His kind heart, gentle nature, and polite manners made him the envy of mothers everywhere. Moshe wasn't satisfied with my dismissive answer, rightly observing the changes in our environment and the increasing vulnerability in which the Jews lived. To me, the changes—even though they could prove dangerous—were somehow exciting. Naively, I didn't internalize the threats to the Jews as a personal fear. I looked into Moshe's eyes and suddenly saw the fear that he felt. I wanted to protect him, shield him from such thoughts—so I did what any immature big brother would do: I shoved him and raced him to the market to run away from the discussion.

Looking back at a panting Moshe as we stormed into the shop, I bumped right into a man walking out. "*Wolf-a-Blinder!* Watch where you are going!" laughed the man. It took me a second to realize that this was my cousin, Jake Grossberg. Moshe and I embraced him. Jake told us that he had finally been released from Polish prison. We paid for our flour, and then the three of us walked back home together.

Prior to the Soviet occupation, Jake had been involved in some illicit communist political activity. Seen as a threat to the Polish government, anyone involved in communist organizing was arrested. Once the Soviets took over, they released Jake from prison and sent him to a sanitarium for a year to recover. Jake and I were close. Seeing him safe was a relief.

On our way home, Jake related his awful experience in prison. It was a lot to take in: Sarah's story about Natasha, now Jake's prison story. Moshe stared absently at his shoes, kicking up dust. I sighed, looking at Moshe. I could see how troubled he was. At that moment, I wished I could take his worry away and bring back the smiling, happy baby brother I knew. I put an arm around him and pulled him closer, showing him a more serious, concerned side than before. He leaned in, keeping his eyes fixed on the dust on his shoes. Jake gave me a questioning look. "He's heard a lot of scary stories," I explained. Jake sighed and nodded sympathetically. Wishing each other *"Gut Shabbos,"* we parted, heading to our respective homes.

Jake was only a few meters away when he stopped, turned, and shouted, "You know, Jabotinsky was right: *Eliminirn di glus oder di glus vet shurli eliminirn ir.* (Eliminate the Diaspora, or the Diaspora will surely eliminate you.)" I had forgotten about that until Jake reminded me. A few years earlier, Zionist leader Ze'ev Jabotinsky had visited our community club, calling on us to establish a Jewish state in the ancestral homeland.

"Eliminate the Diaspora, or the Diaspora will surely eliminate you." Those words echoed in my mind, jarring me from my memories and returning me to our Passover table.

✡

Easing into my seat in silence, I looked around the table. This time it was just the five of us. I missed the raucous family meals we had before 1939. Extended family and guests would fill every corner of our home. My father's eyes would gleam as he recited the story of Passover. My sister would help my mother hide the *afikomen* and tease my brother and me—and all of the younger cousins—when we struggled to find the hidden matzoh. I missed the bountiful meal my mother would prepare and her delicate touch with a gracefully decorated table. I missed Babi Leah—who served as our ruling matriarch for many years. I even missed her sad decline into Alzheimer's, when she would randomly shout "Ooo, fee, fah!" from her rocking chair. I missed our old life.

My father put on a brave face, exchanged a smile with my mother, and started to lead with the ritual prayers. I absently participated, my thoughts wandering. I tried to tell myself that everything would be alright and times would be better. It was just then that Soviet military planes crossed the night sky and cast a solemn silence over us all. My father paused and looked at each and every one of us. He then mouthed to heaven, "G-d only knows if we will be together next Passover."

Chapter 2:
War

Soviet rule had brought a strange new normal. We lived in a constant state of uneasiness. Our culture was reduced to little more than a whisper. The Soviets smothered all public display of our religious practice and communal life. Our daily lives were as stale as communist bread. Still, we felt a wary sense of security. It was most likely better than under German rule, and certainly better than all-out war. As shallow as this optimism was, it offered some hope, some basis to believe that things would work out for the best. We relied on this hope as a foundation to live our daily lives, but each passing week brought another crack in this foundation, threatening to topple our history and existence.

In late April, a large crack appeared. I was playing soccer with my friends on a perfect spring day. As the sun edged through the blossoming tree branches in the late afternoon, we heard the sound in the distance. It was a thunderous rumble, low and slow at first, then rising, rhythmic. There were hundreds, then thousands, of Soviet soldiers marching westbound toward the German border. We stood there, gaping, transfixed by the sheer magnitude of the force.

These poor boys—hungry, thirsty, exhausted. Some appeared to sleep as they marched. Their shoes were in tatters. The procession of soldiers continued through the evening, into the morning, and for the next several days. I shrugged, ambivalent. Surely, with such a massive military presence, the security of Soviet territory was all but guaranteed. I didn't focus on the details, but I should have. I would have realized how hollow the Soviet defense was; these poorly equipped peasants streaming through Dubno would be no match for a technically superior army. One glance at these soldiers would all but invite a German invasion. The signs were all there, but I was young and I didn't recognize them.

We ran home to tell our parents about the sight of the marching soldiers. Everyone had seen them. Like me, my peers thought that no one would challenge such an awesome display of force. Our mothers and fathers, however, felt otherwise. Each wave of Soviet soldiers stirred a quiet panic within Jewish households: War was coming. It made sense, of course. Why would so many soldiers be mobilized if not to engage in active combat?

Contingency plans were prepared. Families bartered material possessions, each household doing their best to predict what they would need in case of war. My father went to see Mudrik, among other former business partners. Ukrainian criminals were assaulting and stealing from random travelers, making the roads dangerous. Stories spread of Jews mugged and beaten on their way to visit relatives in nearby towns. Dubno City Hall was commandeered by the military, leaving next to no municipal services or conduits of public information. Amid the buzz of military activity, Dubno became an eerily still place. And in this precarious environment, Ukrainian bandits seeped into the town from their forest or village dwellings to terrorize the Jews. People were fearful of leaving their homes; people were fearful of staying in them.

Throughout June, 1941, candles burned through the nights as the threat of war loomed. I was restless. Despite the risks, I rode my bike around town throughout the day to meet with friends. I talked into the night on our porch with my cousins. Few in Dubno slept soundly, and whispers about what to do filled every home.

Then, it happened.

The siren began with the long, slow, distant wail. Every soul in Dubno held their breath. Silence. Farmers stopped their plows. Nervous villagers froze in stride. Crowds of people seeking information in the city hall fell silent, hushed by the rhythmic ring of the siren. Desperate eyes searched the sky.

It was June 22, 1941. Reports crackled over the radio, and panic gripped every home. It began. Germany invaded. Families gathered around stereos, nervously listening to the updates. Young boys dashed from one home to the next, informing their relatives and friends about the impending German attack. With frightened eyes, my parents held us close and spoke to us with reassuring words. Moshe and Sarah huddled closer with my parents, while I leaned in close to the radio. It was strange: I wasn't afraid; I was curious, even excited. Surrounded by scared relatives and friends, I felt oddly immune to the rising danger, untouched by the fear that consumed Dubno's Jews.

The Germans attacked Russian bases and military targets, destroying the Dubno airport. Bombs crashed, sirens wailed, and hundreds of frightened citizens ran through the streets with their hands cupped over their noses and mouths, screaming, "Gas, gas!" While this time the bombs did not release gas, smoke and dust from shattered debris and charred rubble permeated the air—creating a noxious-smelling fog.

Stepping out of my house, I craned my neck to sneak a peek from the safety of our porch at the dogfights crisscrossing the sky above.

How little I knew. It was surreal. Embers smoldered in nearby fields, and an orange haze draped the line of trees in the distance, blurring the horizon. In the breaks between the clouds and pillaring smoke, planes, like fireflies, appeared in all directions. Streaking bullets like lightning bolts exploded in supernovas. The Soviet pilots fought honorably but hopelessly. I watched as several Soviet pilots—overwhelmed and outmatched by the technologically superior German planes—deliberately crashed into German fighters. It was simply not enough. It was a not a battle. It was conquest.

Chapter 3:
The Origin of Guilt

June 23, 1941. Military sorties continued overhead in the early morning, and Ukrainian bandits on horseback persisted to lurk around the fringes of the town. No one slept. At dawn I went to City Hall in search of news, only to find the building deserted. Wandering out of the building, I noticed four Ukrainian riders smirking in my direction. They spat menacingly through their mustaches as their horses fidgeted on the cobblestone. Feeling their glares on me, I decided to leave Dubno as soon as possible to see what safer havens might await in Soviet territory. My mind was racing. On the walk home, I kept thinking about the sheer number of Soviet soldiers that had streamed through Dubno. Surely all those troops would be capable of staving off an attack. I stopped by a few friends' houses on my way back to see who was willing to join me. Every home was racked with worry and commotion.

When I arrived home, I found my mom awake, busy packing a suitcase for Sarah. My father planned to take her to Mudrik later in the day. Poor Sarah. She was biting at her fingernails, and her puffy eyes were still wet from the tears. I walked up to her and placed my hand supportively on her back. She turned toward me and bawled. I held her as she cried, her tears spilling onto my shirt. Sarah sobbed about how scared she was to be at Mudrik's and how she couldn't trust Natasha. Of course, she was right. How could she trust anyone? There was no guarantee that she would be safer with a Ukrainian business partner than with her own family. I tried to calm her down, fumbling for words to reassure her that she wouldn't be gone long. She just sobbed and sobbed, soaking the collar of my shirt. I held her tighter, feeling her soft curls brush against the side of my face.

Moshe walked in from outside, where he'd been helping my father tie down a few belongings. He was always the most protective of our big sister, so when he saw how upset she was, he came over to take my place in consoling her. I gave Sarah a small squeeze and patted her again on the back—as though everything would be alright.

"I'm going to Kremenets," I declared to my parents. Kremenets was a city on the way to the old Russian border where I hoped to learn something useful and return to my family within a day or two at most. Hearing me, my mother stopped what she was doing, paused, and looked at me awhile before she spoke. I could see the pain in her eyes and the understanding in her face. She approached me and said, "*Aoyb ir vet zayn hungerik du zalst nisht zeyn farshemt tsu fregn far esnvarg.* (If you are hungry, do not be ashamed to ask for food.)"

At that moment, I remembered all of my mother's kindness. How she often cared for the needy and took in strangers for the Sabbath. Her words seemed to extend a prayer for others to provide for her child where she could not. She pulled out my leather coat from the closet, and even though it was hot, she said that I might need it on cold nights. She embraced me and turned back to helping Sarah. My father had meanwhile come inside. He reached into his pocket and handed me a small stack of neatly folded bills to help me along the way. I thanked him and shouted back as I walked out the door that I'd return in a couple days.

I darted down the street on my bicycle to my friend Pircus's house. Before I had a chance to knock at the door, his mother stormed out, shaking her hand at me. "If you want to go, then go, but leave him alone," she said. The three of us were all talking over one another. I explained that I was just going to Kremenets—a short trip—one day there, one day back. Pircus tried to settle his mother down while she shouted blessings and curses and hopes and fears. After a minute of this, I relented, apologized, and backed away from the house. Just as I settled back on my bicycle, Pircus trotted out despite his mother's pleas, grabbed his bike from against the side of the house, and sped off with me.

We had barely reached Dubno city limits when I realized that I had left my identification and work permits on our kitchen table. We turned around and raced back to my house. There was commotion and activity everywhere. As the day brightened toward noon, the summer heat filled the streets. Young men were all making hurried decisions. There were tears, arguments, and tormented families—all afraid. We weaved around these people, our neighbors, and pulled up to my house.

My father and sister had left a few minutes before I burst in through the front door. My mom was crying over Sarah's departure, and my brother was consoling her. He was a real *mensch*, my brother. I announced that I had forgotten my paperwork, slapped my hand on the documents, slid them off the table, and folded them into my pocket. I went back out the front door, promising again to be back soon.

Marching toward my bicycle, I heard the door bang shut behind me. Pircus and I righted our bikes and started to push off. Suddenly, the front door to my house swung wide open, and my brother leaped off the porch toward us begging, "*Nameh ana rameh.* (Take me on the frame of the bike.)" Moshe felt alone and scared. Trembling, he implored, "*Nameh ana rameh, nameh ana rameh.*" We could hear the desperation in his voice. Pircus looked at me and shrugged. Moshe was a kid. He would be better off safe at home than riding off into uncertainty. Plus, I'd be back in a couple days. I waved him off and told him to go back inside. He was dejected, but I was in a rush and couldn't really expect to make it to Kremenets and back in a couple days with him weighing down the bike. So, we sped off out of Dubno.

I've regretted that choice my entire life—even though I know I probably shouldn't punish myself. With my sister's tears still wet on my shirt and the pleas of my brother ringing in my ears, I left. *I left them.* How was I supposed to know that I'd never see them again?

We weren't alone. Hundreds of young men had the same idea. Pedaling, we chatted with acquaintances who were also traveling in search of answers. There were questions, opinions, hopes—but no answers.

Pircus and I rode through the afternoon into the lingering daylight of a summer evening, crossing three bridges along the way. Bridges became spontaneous gathering points, crowded with people looking for relatives, friends, and the latest war news. At each bridge we met up with someone we knew from Dubno, until there was a small group of us traveling together: Itzchik the cobbler, Bider the baker, and Abraham the teacher.

At dusk, we were stopped at an impromptu checkpoint by a Soviet officer who refused to let us pass. Just as we were about to begin arguing with him, Leib, one of the members of our group, recognized the officer and approached him quietly. After a minute of conversation, the officer looked us over and waved us all through. As luck would have it, this officer had assisted Leib's brother's release from Polish detention for participating in communist activity several years before. Once we were out of earshot of the officer, Leib admitted that he'd lied to him. "I just said that we were all involved in communist activity and punished for it," Leib told us. "He took pity on us." We all laughed and thanked him for his quick thinking. It was well into the night by the time we arrived at Kremenets. We all dispersed in the darkness to find some shelter. Tired, but still feeling the adventure, I found an abandoned shack and slept.

I woke in the morning to the sound of farm animals clanking about in a nearby barn. I smacked myself awake with water from a nearby pump and strolled into the city center. I was eager for news, anything to take back to Dubno to reassure my family, my brother, that things were going to be fine.

Kremenets seemed just as chaotic as Dubno: people milling about, harried efforts to pack carts and horses, pleas to stay, and anguished goodbyes. Searching for posted bulletins, I learned nothing. It was too hard to sift any reliable facts from the ever-evolving rumors that multiplied throughout the city center. Amid the cacophony and confusion, I found my cousin Jake Grossberg, who was returning from L'vov and headed for Dubno. As Jake and I were talking, preparing to return to Dubno with nothing useful to report, a familiar face ran up to us. It was Yasha Groinim, a friend of ours from Dubno who had reached Kremenets in the early morning. He informed us that the road to Dubno was closed at one of the bridges and he was one of the last few people who'd managed to get across the bridge. Jake and I looked at each other, mulling our few options. There weren't any answers, but the one constant rumor was that the Germans were coming. Since it was impossible to learn anything in Kremenets, we agreed to press ahead a little further to the old Russian-Polish border.

The mass of people on the roads was swelling. It was too early for panic, but the tension was as palpable as the humidity. The crowds slowed our progress to the old Russian border. It took most of the morning to make the journey, and when we arrived, we encountered a growing queue of people denied entry into Soviet territory. The overwhelmed guards said that no one would be permitted to enter Russia proper without Soviet-authorized travel papers. This time, I was lucky! I huddled my cousin and friends behind me and presented my work permit and identification to a flustered border guard. Seeing the travel stamp, he waved us through and returned to his hapless enforcement role.

As we distanced ourselves from the commotion behind us, my

cousin and friends slapped me on the back and laughed, wanting to know how I'd managed to get us across. Chuckling with relief, I promised to tell the story when we got the chance. As we pushed on, we came across an old Jewish man who asked us where we came from. When I told him we were from Dubno, he said he had a good friend who lives there: Nussen Kogul. I laughed and told him that Nussen was my father. "Wolf?" the man deduced, clasping his hands together. Elated, he invited us to his house, which was just a few kilometers east of the old Russian border.

The old man killed a couple chickens, and we all helped to prepare an evening meal. He poured us each a drink to toast, and while we were cooking, Jake nudged me: "Nu, how did you have that paper?" As the chickens roasted, we all sat under the shade of a large tree, and I explained how I'd received the travel stamp.

✡

In the spring of 1940, life under the Soviet system retained no semblance of what we'd known before. I was restless—looking to do something, anything. Walking by the city hall one day, I noticed an advertisement on a bulletin board to work on a fishing boat off Crimea on the Black Sea during the summer for three months. The ad promised good pay and accommodations. All one needed to do was register at the city hall and arrive by 8:00 a.m. at the train station with ID and a packed bag. Over the next few weeks, I mulled over the idea and kicked it around with a few friends. Some were also interested, but most suspected that their parents would not approve, especially given the dangers of being a Jew in a time of rising political tension. I figured that if I told my parents in advance, they would find a way to stop me from going. So, I decided not to tell them until the last moment.

The night before the train departed for the fishing boat, we sat down for dinner. I told my mother and father about the ad and all of the benefits. They were both dismissive of the idea. "I'm going," I insisted. My mother was particularly upset because she feared for my safety. But I was 18 years old, I'd been working, and I couldn't stand being in Dubno anymore. I needed to do something new.

The following morning, Sarah and Moshe hugged me goodbye. My mom shook her head in disappointment and kissed me, telling me to be careful. My father then walked me to the train station. There was already a small group of men waiting in line to sign in. A portly older man with bright red cheeks and a broad toothless smile greeted each of the young men. He told them they would need to present their ID so that the Soviet labor official would authorize their work permit. Once they received their permit, they parted from their loved ones and boarded their train—off on an adventure. My father hugged me, slapped me playfully on the cheek, and told me to take care of myself.

That's how I received the stamp!

On the train, I met four other young men from Dubno, as well as others from neighboring towns. We all became fast friends. The journey to the Black Sea took all day, covering more than 1,000 miles of Ukrainian villages and farmland. Still, time passed quickly as I chatted with the others. We talked about the adventure of getting away from hometowns, of meeting girls near the sea, and exploring the black market. Weary, we finally reached our destination and emerged into a dense, salty mist. The cool sea air was welcome and refreshing. Industrial machinery was humming, packaging the daily haul of fish.

We were a diverse group, hailing from all across the ethnic tapestry of Soviet republics. After introducing himself to us, Sasha, a young but experienced sailor, directed us to an open warehouse with cots and a kitchen where the men could grab a meal and get some sleep before starting work the next day. We took some time to wander around the ships and warehouse. The romantic notion of work out on the sea was quickly dispelled by the rotten conditions. Rancid odors wafted across oil-slicked docks. The bunks on the ships were decrepit, rusting from lack of maintenance. Moreover, as groups of workers poured into the warehouse staging area from the train station, it soon became apparent that there was not enough space for everybody. Many of us would be sleeping on the floor.

The following morning, after an awful night's sleep, I rose, excited for the change of pace. Sasha had breakfast ready for us. He told us we'd be divided into teams of six, each headed by a team leader. We would then be assigned a boat and make preparations to head out to sea the next day. Misha, a longtime fisherman, randomly selected me and five other young men for his team. He had been running fishing crews for more than 10 years. He had salt and pepper hair, an unwieldy moustache, and a piercing stare. Crow's feet at the corners of his eyes attested to a jovial spirit and a sense of humor. So, following a series of laughs, Misha began on what appeared to be a serious note. He pulled out a picture of 20 young men who had worked in years past. His solemn tone hushed the small groups as they searched the faces of the smiling young men in the photos.

"Look at these men," Misha said ominously. "Remember their faces. These are men just like you who came here to work, and all drowned in the deep Black Sea waters." No one said a word, and a couple of men gasped and gulped. Just when Misha knew he had instilled the fear of G-d in the men, he cracked a smile, slapped me on the back, and laughed—adding a few more laugh lines to his weathered face and drawing nervous laughter from the group. (I laughed more when I found out that all of the other team leaders had played some version of the same joke on their teams.)

One day during our first week out to sea—our small boats dragged nets to catch sardines—the captain called for the boat to hold. Uri, a mousy and wiry young man, tossed an anchor overboard and was horrified when he realized that his leg was caught in the chain. He screamed for help as the chain pulled taut and the anchor plummeted toward the sea floor. The force of the chain yanked Uri to the floor as he was dragged toward the bow of the ship. Instantly, others grabbed him before he went over and managed to free him from the chain. Panting and pale, Uri trembled. Others breathed deep sighs of relief. I laughed. It's terrible, I know; I shouldn't have laughed. It's just that back then everything was a game. I hadn't learned how dangerous the world could be.

✡

My sea story allowed us a much-needed break from our uncertain predicament. Finally, as the last rays of light peered through the thickets and trees, we inhaled the scent of roasted chicken. The old man, seeing our camaraderie and fearing war, declared he'd join us on our way east.

I sat on my leather coat, reclining against a tree. We sat in a circle around a wonderfully simple bounty spread out before us on a quilt: roasted meat—piping hot and beading succulent juices—black rye bread, freshly picked tomatoes and cucumbers. The old man, more religiously observant than the rest of us, led us in a prayer of thanks for the food. He even managed to surprise us with an old bottle of red wine, just enough to pour a half cup for each of us. Jake sliced the oversized loaf into thick slabs, letting each piece fall gently to its side. Using the bread to soak up the fat of the meat, I held my first piece of warm food since leaving Dubno.

Just as I opened my mouth to take a bite, artillery fire exploded, crackles coming from all directions. The old man, smiling across from me, was shot in the back of the head and fell lifeless in front of me. I was paralyzed. I had never seen anyone shot or killed before. My eyes were fixated on the blood splattered over our picnic. My hand hovered over my lap, still holding the greasy meat in my fingertips. I tried to speak but could only muster a few mumbles. Activity swirled around me in a blur: My friends jumped, scrambled, and kicked up dust in all directions; no one knew which way to go. Jake noticed me sitting stunned and pulled me out of my trance.

I blinked and focused on my bicycle. It was on the other side of the old man's yard, but I couldn't get to it safely. Bullet pings shattered the trees, and bark splintered all around me. I was sitting on my leather coat. I twisted to my feet and swiveled my head around in all directions. It felt as if the wave of a powerful storm was crashing upon us and the only hope we had was to run to shore. I glanced back at my bicycle as bullets chewed the tree leaves above my head. Ducking down, I noticed my leather coat, just out of arm's reach. I turned my head from the coat and started to move away from the eruption of bullets and noise. Some powerful force pulled me back toward the coat; I saw my mother's face and remembered the look in her eyes as she'd handed me the coat. I just couldn't leave it behind. I darted back a step, sliding on the dirt, and crouched to grab my coat.

A mass of retreating Soviet soldiers, civilians, and various farm animals came careening from around the bend in the road. From beyond the line of trees in the distance, German soldiers were advancing—shooting, shelling, and destroying everything in their path. We literally ran for our lives. My leather coat, which I held in my hand as I ran, was pierced by a bullet. Leib, who'd saved us by helping us clear the first checkpoint, was running next to me. All of a sudden, he fell forward and screamed in agony. He latched onto my coat, pulling me down. He pleaded for help, saying that he was shot in his back. I'll never forget the fear in his eyes. "Please, Wolf! I don't want to die! I don't want to die!" Leib lost his strength and crawled. I was torn. I called out to my friends to help me, but I couldn't carry Leib. Injured people fell to the ground and were trampled. Several people fell on Leib, trapping him under their weight. At any moment, I too would have been crushed by the fleeing mass of humanity. "I'm sorry, I'm sorry," was all I could say. I pulled away from Leib, breaking his hold of my leather coat. I was in complete shock. With the blood of the old man on my cheek and Leib's cries in my ears, I forced myself to run as fast as I could, hoping my heartbeat and panting breath would drown out the sounds in my mind.

The thunderous crackles of gunfire continued behind us, propelling the bullets between us and into the dirt and foliage. Staying ahead of the fallen, several Soviet officers on horseback galloped by us in hasty retreat. I remember making eye contact with one officer. He raised his riding whip and shouted encouragement at us, urging us to run for safety. We ran well into the night until the terrorizing sounds subsided in the distance behind us.

We were lucky to have escaped this initial attack. After the war, I learned that a few days after we fled east from Krements, the Germans took over the region. Within a couple months, the Germans murdered nearly 1,000 Jewish men, women, and children. During the next year, 19,000 Jews from Kremenets and nearby towns were penned in a ghetto and deprived of sufficient food, water, and sanitation. In July 1942, Jews of Kremenets mounted an armed resistance, which was ultimately unsuccessful. By August 1942, the Germans had murdered all of the Jews in the ghetto.[iii]

Chapter 4:
Running for Our Lives

There were thousands of people fleeing. Soldiers. Peasant farmers. Mothers dragging children. Old men struggling to carry heavy loads. Refugees. I was part of a mass exodus desperately trying to stay ahead of the German invasion. My group from Dubno managed to stay together. Jake, Groinim, and I arrived together. We found Bider, Pircus, Abraham, and Itzichik soon after.

Don't ask me how they did it, but the Germans planted mines and bombs along the road east to Starokostiantyniv, making the escape that much more perilous. Pircus shook every time a bomb exploded ahead of us, fearing that we too would be killed by an errant step. Planes, motors whirring, constantly hummed above us, spraying bullets.

We ran through the night, throughout the next day, and into the following night. Only adrenaline propelled us on, past the point of complete exhaustion. Panting as we arrived near the outskirts of Starokostiantyniv, we each hunched over and made our way down to a riverbed. Collapsing near the gurgling stream, we plunged our faces into the cool, flowing water and drank until our sides ached. Other survivors of the advancing attack slowly made their way down as well to quench their cotton-mouthed thirst. Nearby, Soviet soldiers led their horses to the swelling pools. Raising my head from the rushing water, I splashed my face and neck, turning away from the water to the riverbank. Looking up, I locked eyes with a Soviet officer; we both paused, searching one another's faces. Suddenly, his eyes lit up in recognition. He raised his telltale riding whip and shouted, "*Malatzi, ribyata!* (Well done, young men!) Here I was on horseback, and you made it all this way by foot."

Starokostiantyniv appeared to be relatively stable, compared to the chaos of the past few days. As I wandered through the empty streets at night, dim candlelight and hushed discussion indicated that every household was awake making preparations. We made our way to the central train station and found some wooden benches to lie on and get a few hours rest. Drifting off that night, I tried to wrap my mind around what was happening. All I wanted to do was explore the excitement, learn something meaningful, and return to my family with some news—and hopefully a plan. A pit of anxiety began to grow in my stomach as I struggled to figure out how I would be able to get home.

A train whistle jarred us from a sleepless night to face another day of uncertainty. Running my dirty hands through my coarse hair, I began to massage my stiff neck. Eyes bloodshot with fatigue, we staggered over to the train schedule to figure out our options. As we perused the table, a familiar voice called out, "Wolf, Jake, Pircus!" We collectively raised our heads and smiled in surprise. We were all friends with N'chemyeh but hadn't seen him much during the past year. He rushed over and embraced us, relieved to see us alive. N'chemyeh said that he'd come to Starokostiantyniv to stay with family for Passover a few months ago. His aging relatives needed his help, and he had agreed to stay for a while, but he desperately wanted to return to his family in Dubno. N'chemyeh invited us over to his relatives' home for a meal.

N'chemyeh's aunt and uncle lived in a small flat near the city center. The stairs had become too difficult for the elderly couple to climb regularly, and their only son, N'chemyeh's cousin, imprisoned a year prior, was unable to help care for them. N'chemyeh, being the *mensch* that he was, had offered to help care for them for a few months until his cousin returned or until he could find alternative care. As we walked into the apartment, we noticed the dismay on the faces of N'chemyeh's aunt and uncle. We suddenly realized how dirty we must have looked. N'chemyeh introduced us to his aunt, who kindly invited us to wash up and offered us tea, bread, and jam. As we took turns in the washroom, N'chemyeh peppered us with questions about Dubno, our journey, our plans. We relayed the details in between mouthfuls of sticky bread, hardly believing our own experience. N'chemyeh was shocked to hear about the flight from Kremenets. Undeterred by the danger of heading west, he planned to depart for Dubno as quickly as possible in order to reunite with his family.

By midday, we were ready to resume our trek eastward. We thanked N'chemyeh's aunt and uncle for their hospitality; they smiled at us weakly with sad eyes and wished us well. As we filed out of their home, N'chemyeh and I lingered together for a few moments outside the threshold of the apartment. Anxiety crossed his face. I invited him to join us, offering an uncertain solace that at least he wouldn't be alone in this unfolding madness.

N'chemyeh shook his head; he was determined to return to Dubno—and our story prompted him to depart more hastily than planned. I nodded, understanding, thoughts drifting toward my loved ones as N'chemyeh stared pensively toward our friends standing outside. I turned to him and hesitated, unsure of what my next words should be. I pursed my lips and then exhaled and said, "If you make it to Dubno, please find my parents and tell them I'm alright." Sensing the gravity of my helplessness and concern, he placed a comforting hand on my should, looked me confidently in the eyes, and promised he would. We embraced once more, he patting my back and saying, "*Zei gezunt.* (Be well.)" I wished him the same and walked out to join my friends.

I never saw N'chemyeh again and never learned of his fate, but believe to my core that he lived to fulfill his promise to me—something I'll explain later.

Our little group wandered back to the train station to try to figure out what to do. Staring once again at the schedule, we realized quickly that most of the trains were canceled, and those still scheduled to depart were unpredictable. Here we were, standing in the middle of thousands of Soviet soldiers and distressed civilians swarming in all directions, following orders, looking for safe passages, seeking food, bartering goods, and agonizing over the future. All we knew was we needed to get out of there, and running on foot was not fast enough.

We finally found a train that was scheduled to depart eastward to Kiev. So, we boarded it, and waited—for hours. Jake was next to me, while some of the others hopped off to look for newspapers or a radio. My anxiety slowly succumbed to the warmth of the train car, and I fell asleep. I may as well have been anesthetized, because the crash and the explosions didn't wake me up.

The Germans bombed our train. Jake shook me fiercely until I finally awoke in a daze. Alarms were ringing. He was screaming. Smoke filled the air. Lucky for us, we sat in the rear train cars. The Germans had destroyed the first half of the train, but there was no guarantee that another bomb wouldn't target the rest. My senses finally started to function, and Jake's words began to sink in. We needed to run, now! We darted from the train. Inside the station, mayhem reigned.

Shouts and gunfire came from all directions. My mind struggled to comprehend the images around me: bodies twisted among mangled metal train parts; rubble and blood mashed into distorted, chaotic sculptures. Among the screams, fires erupted, sending pillars of black smoke into the air.

We crouched under the train and peered between boxcars toward an open field and, in the distance, a line of trees. Jake and I shouted to each other, weighing the risk of making a run for it. We'd be running in the open, but then again, not near any structures that could be bombed. Another German bomb hit the station. The impact surged us forward and onto the stones of the rail bed. We pulled ourselves together and crawled away from the station to the edge of the field.

Jake and I searched for our friends amid the thousands of people running pell-mell in all directions, but it was impossible to see anything clearly. The sound of sirens and gunfire was deafening. Seeing no other choice, we started to run. We sprinted as fast as we could through the field, imagining a hail of bullets raining down on us at any moment. We made it to the trees, and only then stopped to look back. Starokostiantyniv was ablaze under waves of German aerial attacks. We stood there a few moments to try to comprehend what we were watching. Jake and I looked at each other in disbelief. It was a frighteningly efficient devastation. With the sun setting behind us, we oriented ourselves and walked toward the darker horizon and hopefully to safer places.

Again, it was only after the war that I learned how close I came to being swallowed by the German advance. On July 8, 1941, just weeks after this initial assault, the Germans occupied Starokostiantyniv. As soon as the Germans arrived, they tortured the town's Jewish population. In late August 1941, the Jews of Starokostiantyniv were concentrated in a ghetto with other Jews from nearby towns, including Gritsev, Ostropol, and Staraya Sinyava. By November 1942, the Germans had murdered more than 7,000 Jews.[iv]

Chapter 5:
Refugee

The road to Kiev took a toll on all of us. Just outside of Starokostiantyniv, we encountered Groinim and Itzchik, followed soon thereafter by Pircus and Bider in succession. We were all relieved to see each other, but Abraham hadn't turned up, and none of us knew where he was. It was only well after the war, when I first visited Israel, that I learned that Abraham had survived. At the time, it was difficult to accept that our friends had died. So, we didn't even think about it. We just ran away from danger.

We walked until the sky was ink black and painted with stars. Along with hundreds, maybe thousands, of others, we pushed ourselves past the point of exhaustion as we trudged forward toward the Soviet border. Many chose to rest on the side of the road, sleeping exposed and vulnerable.

After walking for hours, we came across an abandoned farm. Whoever lived there must have left in a hurry, because there were a number of belongings—saddles, tools, dishes, fabric—strewn about the grounds, apparently too cumbersome for the owners to take. Then again, there was always the chance that the owners may return. Despite the risk, we all agreed that we needed to rest, at least for a few hours. So, we found the stable and plopped in the mounds of hay and instantly fell asleep.

We slept until we were abruptly awakened by a screaming rooster. Not long after, we discovered four horses grazing in the pasture. The farm seemed abandoned, but we didn't have time to consider the ethical consequences of stealing the horses. We needed to keep moving, and these horses offered the best way to get as far away from the Germans as possible. They were stubborn horses, but Groinim, who had worked on a farm in Dubno, managed to overcome their resistance and saddle them with an experienced touch. It was an incongruously beautiful morning. Yes, we were fleeing for our lives from the Wehrmacht—but dew frosted the overgrown grass as the sun sparkled through the line of trees serving as a windbreak. Butterflies danced on flower petals and chirping birds fluttered among the branches of the large oaks. The air was cool and refreshing. Easing onto my horse, I pressed my heels down, just as Groinim instructed.

We started off with a bouncing trot, but eventually found the comfortable canter, striding gallantly along a dirt path. For a brief moment, I was happy—out for a ride on my horse! As my confidence in the saddle grew, the horse trusted me more and began to speed up. The rhythmic hoofs struck the ground so fast that one step became indistinguishable from the other. I held the reins, squeezed my thighs against the horse's sides, and shouted for the horse to go. With a jolting burst, the horse sped into a cruising gallop. The wind whistled in my ears, and I laughed with pure joy. The fields and trees zipped by in a blur, and my eyes watered, squinting to see the road in front of me. For those fleeting minutes, I forgot myself; life was peaceful and good.

Racing at breakneck speed, I felt increasingly out of control. I eased my horse back to a slower pace. I looked around and realized that I had recklessly left my friends behind me. Pircus, who rode the most stubborn animal on the planet, struggled to get his horse to go in the right direction. Groinim rode side by side with him, just to make sure that the horse didn't dart off. Jake did his best to keep up with me but couldn't bring himself to ride at full gallop. After I stopped and waited awhile, they finally caught up and chided me for racing ahead. I smiled and blamed the horse. My cheeks hurt from giddy laughter, and tears of joy streamed down the creases of my squinting eyes; that moment was wonderful.

My mental reprieve was short-lived. We were quickly reminded where we were and why we needed to keep moving. Aircraft mortars erupted in the clear blue sky above. Squadrons of Soviet planes, like migrating birds, glided west, the blinding midday sun obscuring their approach. We could feel the pressure building behind us. Explosions in the distance signaled that we didn't have much time until the bullets would again be streaking by us.

The roads were increasingly cluttered and congested, thousands of people fleeing, wandering. We did our best to keep moving, but the German machines were too fast and the Soviet resistance too weak. The rumbling of military equipment droned on—tanks, jeeps, planes. Tank shell explosions rocked the earth behind us, like a giant monster stomping louder with every step. We passed hundreds of peasants, each dragging their livelihoods in weathered wooden carts. No matter how fast we rode, we couldn't seem to put enough distance between us and the advancing German front.

We passed countless Soviet soldiers doing their best to organize and find some stable footing to mount a resistance. But, like a fighter defending himself on his heels, the Soviet army kept slipping further and further back. At our best, we managed to stay just ahead or even with the Soviet retreat.

As the sun dipped lower, mortar shells crashed louder and closer. There was nowhere to hide, and at the rate we were going, we'd be ensnarled in the front line in less than an hour. Much less, as it turned out.

It happened in an instant. The shell crashed on the edge of a field to our left with an eruption of dirt and wheat that showered down on our fallen bodies. The shock of the impact sent us all to the ground in a haphazard tumble. At first, I had no idea if I was dead or alive. My ears were ringing, and there was smoke everywhere. Just a moment before, I was weaving around a wheelbarrow—and then everything went loud and black. When my eyes were able to focus again, I noticed the wheelbarrow was upside down, its contents strewn across the dirt. I could see people writhing and shifting but could hear only the ringing in my ears. I started to shout for my friends and reached wildly in all directions, seeking their familiar faces.

First I saw Pircus. He was sooty but seemed fine otherwise. He kept talking to me, mouthing his words emphatically, but I couldn't make out a sound. Groinim was crawling toward us, rubbing the dirt away from his eyes. We were caught in the middle. Soviet soldiers, running from the Germans, waved their guns blindly behind them, shooting in the opposite direction. It was a miracle we weren't hit by a stray bullet. The explosions intensified. We feared we'd be run over by German tanks at any moment.

Then Groinim saw it. Our only hope. A cargo train slowed to change tracks, giving us a narrow window to survive. Pircus and Groinim stumbled to their feet, holding their hands over their heads to shield themselves from the falling debris. But where was Jake? I couldn't slow them down. I still couldn't hear a thing. I was trapped inside a terrifying silent movie. I scurried through the smoke looking for Jake. I crawled over bodies, some dead, some alive. Shattered wood lay everywhere.

It was the shivering that drew my attention. Jake was nearest the explosion, lying in a ditch near the edge of the field. He held himself, shaking. I couldn't hear him, but his lips quivered, and his eyes were full of panic. I shouted at him to get up. He was frozen with fear and wouldn't move. There was no time for this. If we didn't move now, we would die. I grabbed him by his shirt and hoisted him to his feet. It was like dragging a statue, but eventually Jake's legs came to life and moved alongside mine, his arm braced over my shoulder.

Pircus and Groinim were ahead of us. They looked back to see us limping our way over. They shouted at us to hurry. Jake finally noticed the train, snapping him out of his daze. His pace quickened and his arms pumped, showing the striker speed he'd displayed so often on the soccer field. Now, it was I who struggled to keep up with my sprinting cousin. The train was moving, also desperate to outrace the falling bombs.

Pircus spotted an open boxcar, guiding all of us to the rolling haven. We raced with every fiber of our bodies. All of the years cutting school to play soccer were paying off. We were young, fit, and fueled by adrenaline. Pircus helped bring me on board, grasping my forearm and reaching over to pull me by my belt. We collapsed on the floor, hearts pounding. As the train lurched east, we looked back to see the smoldering earth behind us. Worse, of those that managed to evade the gunfire and mortars, we saw hundreds failing to reach the train, collapsing in despair—elderly, children, pregnant women.

A long time passed before anyone said anything. We were literally shell-shocked, sprawled out on the cargo floor, searching silently to make sense of what had just happened. We each sat there, contemplating our fate, watching the Ukrainian countryside pass by. Eventually, someone lit a cigarette, prompting others to do the same. Quiet conversation started up. People cried. Others paced nervously. Some just stared at the fading light of the day, lost in a catatonic trance.

The voices in the boxcar didn't sound right to me. The ringing in my ears subsided, but I could not hear anything from my left ear. Sticking my finger into my ear, I shook the imaginary water out, hoping that somehow it would heal. The sound never came back. It was strange, only hearing from one ear.

I looked around to see what others were doing. Jake walked over with tears in his eyes. He started to thank me for lifting him out of the ditch. I stopped him, putting my arm around his shoulder, thanking him for waking me on the train in Starokostiantyniv. He smiled, and lit two cigarettes, passing one to me. We just sat there, smoking together, staring out into the dusk.

It was late evening by the time the sound of screeching brakes signaled our arrival in Kiev. As the train eased into the station, we began to debate our options. There were no good ones. We had very little money, our clothes and bodies were disheveled and filthy. Our stomachs ached, our throats were parched. We hopped off the train and observed dozens of groups like us, lost.

We didn't have much time to linger near the station. Local police weren't happy with hundreds of dirty people milling around. They paced with batons, chasing people away to loiter somewhere else. Large signs were posted across the city warning that the citizens of Kiev were prohibited from sheltering refugees.

We decided it would be best to break into smaller groups to look for some help and then meet back at the train station by morning. Pircus and Groinim went off together, while Jake and I set out to look for food and water. My mother's parting words echoed in my mind: "If you should be hungry, do not be ashamed to ask for food."

Wherever we walked, doors and windows were shuttered and people on the streets avoided us. Eventually, we found a few Jewish homes, where we begged for shelter, food, and water. Those who answered their doors took pity on us, but their faces were creased with worry, their eyes darting back and forth along the street in each direction. No one would allow us in. They said they were afraid of the police orders. Some shoved bread and butter quickly at us, others scraped a few coins together. Starving, we ate our bread and butter. We found a public water well and drank. Thankfully, it was a warm summer. Jake and I, amongst thousands of other refugees, lay on the streets to sleep. Just as I turned on my side, I noticed the government posters, and a sinking feeling came over me: I am a refugee.

When we woke early the next morning, Kiev was evacuating. Worried families gathered up their belongings and began the long procession to destinations unknown but beckoning with glimmers of hope. Tears and goodbyes echoed through the streets as families parted, some leaving behind elderly or those too weak to travel. Those able to leave were fortunate. We witnessed tens of thousands of Soviet soldiers taking up positions in what appeared to be a robust effort to defend Kiev. However, this too would end up being a failure. Within a couple months of our departure from Kiev, the German army would encircle the city, destroy the Soviet soldiers, and murder every remaining Jew.

Chapter 6:
Trains

Jake and I found the others waiting at the train station, just as we had agreed the night before. They too had slept on the streets and hadn't found much to eat. Standing in the middle of an exodus, we had a choice to make. Trains were still departing, but who knew for how much longer? When would the air raid sirens sound in Kiev? We found a map and huddled around to see where we should go. Either way we would need to head east, but should we go north or south?

People streamed in all directions, filing into crowded train cars. There didn't appear to be a consensus on where people were going. Some planned to move to the outskirts of Kiev, placing their faith in the military's ability to withstand a German attack. Others committed to going much further, deeper into Soviet territory. Some—lugging what seemed like everything they owned—apparently had no intention of ever returning.

Pircus suggested that if we headed north, there would likely be more Soviet troops and military installations capable of resisting the Germans. I disagreed. Yes, it was summer, but we had nothing but the clothes on our backs, and if the war dragged on, we'd freeze in the Russian winter. Unanimously agreeing on this point, we looked for southern options.

We were nervous about the trains; they were easy targets to bomb, and we were sitting ducks. On the other hand, being stuck in the middle of a firefight was far worse, so better to get as far away from the front line as possible. We pooled our money and purchased the cheapest tickets possible to Kharkiv, via Poltava.

Waiting for our train to depart, we learned that the Germans had taken Starokostiantyniv and were advancing toward Kiev. The Soviet army had suffered severe losses, managing only to slow the

German advance long enough for the most able-bodied to escape. Stalin issued a decree: All towns facing capture by the Germans were to be evacuated and burned. Citizens were permitted to take what they could carry but not to leave anything but charred remains behind. The nightmare of a vast Nazi empire in the east was becoming all too real.

After a short delay, we were on our way deeper into Soviet territory. The wheels slipped on the tracks until the friction built up enough to surge the engine forward, jerking each car along behind it. The train was crowded well beyond its capacity, and the rancid smell of thousands of dirty refugees permeated the cabins. Peering out through the windows, we noticed the burning towns. Towers of black smoke climbed from narrow points on the horizon, drifting widely as the ashes were carried off into the atmosphere. Implementation of Stalin's orders appeared to be well underway.

We stopped in Poltava. The train would wait less than an hour before continuing on toward Kharkiv. As we piled out of the train car, I took a deep breath to clear my sinuses of the stench in the coach. It was already starting to get dark, making it that much more difficult to make our way around an unfamiliar town. The only consolation was that everyone else was in the same predicament as us.

Mindful of our limited time, we made the short walk to the town center to see if we could find any food, water, or information. All we found were rumors that a Soviet resistance was building in Rostov-na-Donu. Many in the town were packing, and uniformed police readied torches on the outskirts. Arguments filled the streets about whether the Soviet Army would be able to hold off the Germans. Some opted to stay, overwhelmed at the prospect of leaving their homes.

At this point, we weren't completely starving, so we didn't risk looking for food in abandoned homes for fear of being caught by Soviet police. I tried a few times to offer people help packing their belongings in exchange for a piece of bread but was waved off each time. The others tried the same with similar results. We were on the last train through Poltava. Fearing we'd be stranded, we hurried back to the train and crammed ourselves back inside. Looking out into the evacuating town, a sadness came over me.

Up until this point, despite the danger, I had felt a sense of excitement, of adventure. Poltava was not under imminent attack. Poltava was a medium-sized city that, in the darkness, felt much like a small town. Although the German advance loomed dangerously close, when I walked through the streets, it was calm. It wasn't that the people evacuating weren't worried; angst was etched in their faces. It was the resignation in their eyes; the people of Poltava conceded that they were in all likelihood leaving their homes for good. They did not depart in haste or panic. It was a slow procession of slouched people heaving their belongings into the night to uncertain destinations. I pitied these people. My thoughts couldn't linger on them for long because each time the train swayed, I was crushed by the weight of the people standing in the box car pressing me into the wall.

We finally managed to put a little distance between ourselves and the German advance. As it turned out, many Jews succeeded in leaving Poltava before the German troops entered the city. Unfortunately, a great many others did not. On September 19, 1941, Poltava was occupied by the Germans. Jews were required to wear a Star of David patch and conscripted for forced labor. Anyone disobeying orders was shot. By November 1941, the Germans had killed all 5,000 of the city's remaining Jews.[v]

✡

It should have been a relatively short ride to Kharkiv, but the train made frequent long stops. At each one, angst and speculation spread in proportion to our uncertainty:

"The train is stopping so the Germans won't see the moving target in the night."

"The Germans bombed the tracks."

"The Soviets are blocking the trains."

The conditions on the train worsened with each stop. The small windows let in a slight breeze through the cars when the train moved, but standing still in the sweltering summer heat and humidity, the air in the cars was chokingly putrid.

At last, in the middle of the night, we arrived at Kharkiv. We squeezed out of the train onto the platform, our dirty clothes clinging to our sweaty bodies. This was the end of the train line. All passengers departed. Soldiers banded together, faces sullen, smoking cigarettes, straining under their heavy packs. Civilian refugees staggered around, lost.

Kharkiv was already mostly deserted, save for a few looters scavenging for tradeable goods. The pang of hunger finally struck us. Looking at one another, we started to realize how we must look: exhausted, dirty, hungry. We quickly set off to scour the town for supplies; it was all going to be burned anyway. I found a bag of sugar. Jake found some stale bread. Pircus, linens and bedsheets. Groinim, a box of matches and a set of wooden eating utensils.

Refugees spilled throughout Kharkiv. Some planned to stay the night. Some looted houses, carrying off chairs, rugs, pots. Some wandered toward the outskirts, looking for food in farmhouses. Others just stood on the platform, staring hopefully into the distance waiting for another train. There was nothing to keep us in Kharkiv; staying would only leave us closer to the German invasion. So, we decided to start walking south, staying as close to the train tracks as possible— just in case we could catch another ride.

Not more than an hour passed before the first planes started flying overhead. It was impossible to determine if they were Soviet or German. Either way, we'd learned enough during the past few days to know that whenever there were planes in the air, trouble was coming.

We walked faster, but it was pitch black ahead of us, and we had no idea how much further it would be before we reached another town.

We'd been walking for hours when we finally came upon an industrial depot where a lone cargo train loaded with coal and iron was readying to depart. Generators hummed, casting a glaring light onto the platform where men hurriedly loaded the remaining containers on the train. The Soviet officers responsible for the cargo were anxiously waiting to depart, standing in their trucks and staring off into the distance expecting an attack. Several refugees approached the platform, begging the officers to let them ride to safety. All were beaten back or forced to continue walking as rifle muzzles herded the desperate people away from the platform back onto the fields.

While the soldiers fended off pleading refugees, we—and dozens of others—crept around the dark side of the train and quietly climbed up the rails. The train rocked, and a swell of voices from the platform cried for help. It was heartbreaking. As the train picked up speed, we scrambled to find a ledge in between the train cars or protruding step near the base of a cargo door, anything that provided a secure place to stand and hold on. With the train well underway, the officers abandoned the platform, driving off in the night. The refugees flooded the tracks, chasing after the train car. Not one of them could make it.

The train churned for a couple hours. Standing outside in the chilly night air, the wind cut through our ragged clothes. Wrapping myself in my leather coat, I was thankful that it was summer. It was too dark, too windy, and too loud to notice if any German planes were bombing the ground behind us, just as it was impossible to figure out exactly where we were going. The consensus was that we were generally heading south. By early dawn, we noticed a large river bending to the west. Jake was certain that it was the Dnieper, which meant we were in Dnipropetrovsk.

At the outbreak of war on the Eastern Front, nearly 130,000 Jews lived in Kharkiv. During the summer of 1941, more than 100,000 Jews left the city and headed east—either in the officially organized evacuation or independently. More than 10,000 Jews remained behind in the city and its environs. On October 23, 1941, the Germans occupied Kharkiv. Jews were forced under police guard to move into the barracks of a machinery plant located in the tractor factory zone. They were abused, dispossessed, and forced to sleep outdoors. Many Jews froze to death, and hundreds were murdered. Jews were penned up behind barbed wire in a ghetto that lacked running water, heat, doors, and windowpanes. Guards were posted around the ghetto, and its inhabitants were forbidden to leave. Those that attempted to leave were shot. Food was not supplied and could not be purchased. Women were allotted one hour a day, at noon, to draw water from a well. Many Jews resorted to drinking melted snow. The inhabitants of the crammed barracks were forbidden to evacuate the bodies of the many who died of starvation or disease. Jewish property was looted with abandon, and the Jews were forced to provide the police with warm clothing and supply money for liquor at Christmas-time.[vi]

On December 24, 1941, the Germans killed some 200 mentally ill Jews. On December 26, Jewish volunteers were enlisted for labor in Poltava, Romny, and Kremenchug. Trucks pulled into Kharkiv the following day, and the approximately 500 volunteers were packed aboard, driven out of the city, and murdered. Another 500 Jews were killed between that time and the end of the month. The ghetto was liquidated January 2 through 8, 1942. The ill and the disabled were driven in trucks, while others, guarded by the Waffen-SS and the SD, were marched to the murder site—two large trenches that had been dug at Drobitskii Yar, near the city. The Jews were executed by members of the Schutzpolizei. By the end of 1942, another 64 Jews had been captured and murdered in Kharkiv.[vii]

Chapter 7:
Bridges and Bread

Once our train came to a stop, workers urgently unlocked and opened the cargo bays, slid open the doors of the cars, dropped ramps, and began wheeling off containers to idling trucks. We hopped off, kicking up dust around us, and staggered forward among thousands of people.

Dnipropetrovsk was a beehive of activity. Warnings of an incoming German invasion were broadcast in all directions. Walking toward the central terminal, we heard the roaring rapids of the Dnieper River ahead. Once we reached the terminal plaza, we stood at the railing overlooking the expanse of flowing water and considered how best to cross over to the eastern side. Military personnel stood guard at the bridges, controlling access across. Wading across wasn't an option; the river was too wide and the current too strong.

Planes gleamed high above in the morning light. Our pulses quickened at the sound of their motors. Hours passed, and not one train left. Finally, as evening approached, several trains were preparing for departure. As we waited, I noticed several small groups of teenage boys sitting along a fence with wooden planks in their hands. They appeared to be orphans. It seemed clear that they were waiting for something.

Curious, I walked up to the boys. "What are you doing with the planks?" I asked.

The boys just stared at each other. I wondered if maybe my Russian was worse than I'd thought. Eventually, one of the boys hopped off the fence and said, "I'll tell you about the planks for a cigarette."

Laughing, I produced two cigarettes, struck a match, and lit them both. "Nu, explain," I said, handing the boy his smoke.

"They won't let people clog the bridge," he began, pointing at the crowd massing near the pedestrian bridge. "No one wants to wait, because we hear the planes flying, and everyone is worried the Germans will bomb the bridges." On cue, several planes flew overhead. With our hands shielding our eyes from the sun, we looked up. Thankfully, these were Soviet planes, but the tension increased significantly.

"And the planks..." I prompted.

"Right," he resumed, after blowing a smoke ring. "With the congested bridge, people tried to jump on the moving train, hoping to make it across. But when the train would sway, the people couldn't hold on...and they fell into the river below."

"So why the planks?" I asked again, with rising impatience.

"There hasn't been a train in a while," the boy went on, "but we think there will be at least one more that will cross the rail bridge today. The weight of the cars makes the train unbalanced on the bridges. We are going to use the planks to bridge the gap between the train cars, and hopefully this will keep us from falling off the train."

I smiled and mussed his hair. "Smart kid," I said. Returning to my friends, I suggested that we all find a plank. There was a broken pallet, which we separated, each taking a meter-long plank. Walking toward the platform, we tried to locate a train to ride.

Hours passed, until finally one of the trains started moving. Thousands of people wedged themselves into the train headed eastward across the river. It would have been impossible to control the swarm of people clinging onto the train, and no one attempted to stop them. Jogging alongside the train in the rocky yard, we each managed to find a space in between the cars and crammed between the bumpers. Standing on the end of the bumper, the first shift of the train threw us off balance. The boys were right. We placed the wooden planks underneath us, resting each end of the board on the bumpers.

I leaned my back against the train car behind me, held onto the board underneath me, and then raised my feet up flat against the bumper in front. As the train cars would draw apart and converge again, I would extend or bend my knees to maintain contact with the bumper in front of me.

It was calamitous. Thousands of people surged onto the train, grasping for anything to hold onto. Some climbed up to the top, others held onto protruding handles. The screeching wheels rolled, pulling the train toward the bridge. I felt a mix of hope and dread. Peering out over the Dnieper, I figured that if we could make it across, we'd be safe from the Germans; the river would certainly protect us from the looming advance. Nearing the edge of the bridge, I gasped. Suspended above the tracks, I stared at the space below—just a wooden plank keeping me from falling in between the train cars, through the tracks, and into the dark water below.

The train gradually sped up, creating a rush of wind. The train and bridge creaked and clicked, swaying. People shouted, desperately trying to hold on to overcrowded handlebars. Suddenly, the train dipped low to the right, sending several people from the top tumbling over, plummeting into the water below. I grasped the wooden plank firmly and pressed my back and feet against the bumpers with all my strength. The motion of the train shifted me from side to side, but I managed to stay secure. The train continued to heave to and fro, tossing stowaway refugees into the rapids. It felt like an eternity, but eventually we made it across. My clenched, white-knuckled hands relaxed once I was no longer staring at the abyss of the Dnieper below me.

Just then, air raid sirens wailed, and the train slowed to a crawl. We couldn't see or understand what was happening, but we heard a rush of screaming people. Next, we heard loud clanging, as if someone was banging pots and pans against the train. I hopped off the train and rolled to the ground. The others did the same. Looking back across the river, we couldn't make out much beyond the faint outline of the city, but we could hear the rumble of aircraft, and we noticed what seemed like falling clouds and the eruption of gunfire.

German paratroopers—some disguised as Russian soldiers—blanketed the city, causing mass panic. Bullets raced from every angle and the refugees scrambled in all directions. Civilians and retreating soldiers ran in wild confusion; many were killed, injured, or captured. We had no idea where to go. The train tracks were our best guide, so we started running alongside them, dropping to the ground when the shooting got too close. We ran like this through the night, along with thousands of others. It was frightening and devastating. In the immediate attack, hundreds were killed in the crossfire. Many fell running in the night, injured. Others collapsed in exhaustion.

By the end of August 1941, the Germans had occupied Dnipropetrovsk, home to nearly 90,000 Jews. As in Kharkiv, many, but not all, of the Jews managed to get out. Upon arrival, the Germans immediately began assaulting, raping, and murdering those who remained. Jews were ordered to wear white armbands with the Star of David on their sleeves. By the time the Germans were forced out of Dnepropetrovsk in 1943, they had murdered approximately 20,000 Jews.[vii]

By early light the morning after our flight from Dnipropetrovsk, we were safely away from immediate danger. We stopped briefly at an intersection where people, horses, and trucks all seemed to take over the roads. We had no idea where we were. Thousands and thousands of people streamed in every direction, making it hard to orient ourselves as we tried to figure out which way we should head next. Nearly everyone travelling looked dirty and exhausted. We stood there in the middle, quite literally at a crossroads.

Jake and I looked at one another, overwhelmed by the masses of people flooding the roads and the uncertainty about what to do next. I twisted around, looking for some sign or direction, unable to come up with anything. It was then that Jake asked, "Didn't we hear rumors of a resistance movement at Rostov-na-Donu?" I raised my eyebrows, pleased with this idea that offered a glimmer of hope. Collectively, we began to nod in approval, each one of us remembering hearing something promising about Rostov. Whether or not it was true, the thought of a destination with some stability was motivating to us, as we stood there lost in a crowd of evacuees.

We asked a truck driver for directions to Rostov. He pointed southeast, saying he was going to Donetsk but would make several stops along the way. The trains were all gone, so other than walking, our only other means of transportation was to hop on cargo beds of truck transports. The driver let us hop on his truck but said that we'd need to leave at his next stop. We gratefully accepted the offer and sprawled out, rubbing our sore legs.

There were convoys of overloaded trucks—military, industrial, and civilian—all rumbling east toward safety. The retreat was so chaotic and frantic that most Soviet soldiers didn't prevent the fleeing refugees from hopping on. When chased off one truck, we would run to keep pace with a convoy to hop on another. We continued this way for nearly a week—running and hopping on trucks. When we passed through a town, we would stop just long enough to find scraps of food and water—barely enough to survive.

Haggard, we eventually made it to Rostov-na-Donu. The city appeared largely deserted. Most civilians had either left or were in the process of leaving. The remaining few were protected only by a few disorganized Soviet units. Speaking with some of the remaining civilians, we learned that people from Rostov were dispersing eastward to link up with relatives or friends scattered across the sprawling Soviet interior. Unfortunately, we didn't know anyone or have anywhere to go.

We spent several days in Rostov, sleeping in abandoned homes, searching for food, and smoking with soldiers. We learned that the Germans were advancing swiftly. Reinforcements were coming to Rostov, and the soldiers had received orders prohibiting retreat. Most of the soldiers were busy preparing defensive positions: barricades, barbed wire, and trenches. A sizable number of the remaining civilians labored voluntarily alongside the soldiers pending the arrival of the promised reinforcements.

Increasingly desperate for food, I approached people packing bags and offered my assistance. Just as in Poltava, I was mostly brushed off. However, an older man carrying a suitcase took pity on me. He said that his wife had hurt her leg and he needed a hand loading their belongings onto their cart and helping her aboard. He said they were moving to be with relatives in another town and that if I could help him pack his cart, he would provide me with bread. I was overjoyed and eagerly accepted his offer.

The old man escorted me to his home. As we entered, he introduced me to his wife, who sat on a chair with her leg elevated as she prepared a basket of food for their journey. Arrayed on the table were jars of preserves, loaves of bread, a pile of fresh vegetables, and thick blocks of cheese. My eyes bulged, and when my stomach grumbled, I placed my hand over my belly, embarrassed. The woman looked up at me and her husband inquiringly. He explained to her that I would help him pack the cart and assist her down the stairs. Relieved, she smiled and thanked me. The man then pointed to belongings in their small apartment, noting that they would be taking all but the heavy furniture.

I climbed up and down the flights of stairs to the couples' apartment carrying bundles of housewares and clothes, packing them neatly on the cart. Each time I entered their unit, I needed to force myself to look away from the kitchen to block the hunger pangs from my mind. It took the better part of the morning to finish the job, but the couple was finally ready to go. Hoping to receive the bread soon, I asked the man if there was anything else I could do to help. With his wife smiling from the cart, he said there was one more thing he needed from me and asked me to follow him back into the apartment.

As we walked, the man asked me where I planned to go. I told him that I had no idea, and briefly recounted my perilous journey to Rostov. The man said that if I could make it further south toward Krasnodarsky Krai, there were a number of collective farms that could absorb us and offer us food and shelter in exchange for work. It was the best idea I had heard. I told him I would tell my friends and we would try to make it there before the Germans arrived. The man thanked me for my help, and then made me such a kind offer that I nearly cried.

The man said that he wasn't sure whether or not they would ever make it back to Rostov: Who knew how the war would turn out? So, for as long as I remained in Rostov, he wanted me—and my friends— to stay in his home. He said that I was welcome to the food in the kitchen, wished me well, and walked out the door. Stunned, I turned toward the kitchen and found shelves of tea, bread, preserves, cheese, vegetables, and smoked meat. I tore off a piece of bread and near- ly choked getting it down. Eyes welling with tears, I raced down the stairs to find the man and his wife sitting on their cart, prompting the horses to start. They noticed me in the doorway and turned toward me. I stopped, my heart pounding with gratitude. I raised a weak hand and mouthed, *Thank you*. They smiled and rode away, she rub- bing her husband's arm and looking at him with pride.

I couldn't believe it. I ran back up the stairs and walked through the apartment. Their generosity was incredible; I suddenly realized how the poor felt when my mother took them in and cared for them. I took a few more bites to satiate my hunger, then went out to look for my friends. I managed to find them all and bring them back to the apartment.

We had been fleeing for nearly a month, but standing in the comfort of a home made it feel like I'd been away for years. We were in disbelief: food to eat, a place to clean up, and a roof over our heads. We debated whether or not to stay for fear that the Germans would invade at any moment. It was the usually quiet Itzchik who spoke first. "G-d only knows when we will ever have a place like this again," he said. No one could argue with that logic. It was settled: We knew we wouldn't be able to enjoy this gift for long, but we decided to sleep in Rostov one more night and then depart the following day. Bider and Groinim divided the food into six equal rations as the rest of us found utensils to set the table. The rations were then divided once more equally—half for the night, the rest for the next morning.

Groinim, who was the most observant of us all, said a few prayers over the meal. After our collective "amen," we sat quietly, savoring each bite. I can still remember the delicious combination of the salted cheese and fresh vegetables over the bread, the tomato juice oozing onto the black rye with each bite.

For several minutes, we savored our food in silence. Then I cleared my throat and asked if anyone had heard of Krasnodar Krai. Jake nodded, noting that he'd heard of collective farms in the area. I told the group of the old man's recommendation. Between mouthfuls, we shrugged, all generally agreeing that it made sense to make our way toward a place that could provide us with a place to sleep and eat. What we didn't know was how long and how dangerous the road would be.

The old couple had some soap, so once we finished our rations, we took turns washing ourselves. This was the first chance we'd had in about a month to properly clean up. It felt wonderful to scrub the crusted dirt off our filthy bodies but awful to put back on the rancid clothes. After we all washed up, we gathered around the living room on plush cushions and blankets to get ready for our first peaceful sleep in a long while. Pircus prepared tea for all of us. We sat sipping our drinks and speculating about the fate of our families and the future until our eyelids grew heavy. One by one, we drifted off to sleep.

The next morning, we woke to the sounds of truck engines rumbling through the city. Out of respect for the old couple, we straightened up their place and expressed thanks to their apartment, in the hope that somehow they would hear our gratitude. Putting away the last clean cup, I noticed an old wooden spoon resting on the counter. I picked up the spoon and turned the long handle with my fingers. I decided to take the spoon with me as a reminder that people can be good. We closed the door behind us, walked down the stairs, and into the bright morning light to face another day of uncertainty as we ventured ever further away from home.

As things turned out, we were only a couple months ahead of the mass evacuation. Word about Rostov being a center of resistance had spread quickly throughout the Soviet Union, drawing tens of thousands of refugees. The resistance didn't last long.

From September through November, 1941, the Soviet authorities oversaw a mass evacuation. About 10,000 Jews succeeded in leaving the city during this period. On November 21, 1941, the Germans occupied Rostov. This occupation lasted only about a week. On November 29, the Red Army counterattacked and retook the city. In the short period of their rule in Rostov-na-Donu, the Germans, acting through a local Jewish council, registered the entire Jewish population and forced them to wear yellow Stars of David. About 1,000 Jews were murdered in the city during this brief interval. After the Red Army's liberation of Rostov-na-Donu, many of the Jews who had left the city in the autumn of 1941 returned.[ix]

In the summer of 1942, as the Germans approached Rostov-na-Donu for the second time, another evacuation began. This evacuation was poorly organized, and not many Jews succeeded in escaping before the city was re-occupied by the Germans on July 24, 1942. On August 11, 1942, the Jews of Rostov-na-Donu were rounded up, supposedly for resettlement in the ghetto. Over the ensuing several days, thousands of Jews were taken by truck northwest of the city and either shot or murdered in gas vans. By February 1943, when Rostov was liberated from the Germans for the last time, as many as 30,000 Jews had been massacred.[x]

Chapter 8:
Walking Through the
Wasteland

The road toward Krasnodar Krai took nearly a week of tiring travel, and it would be another week of endless marching across southern Ukraine and the Caucuses before we finally reached a destination. There were thousands of refugees trekking in the summer heat, many struggling under the weight of their household possessions. I passed countless people whose carts had broken down—pleading for help lest they be forced to abandon their worldly goods on the road. Worse yet were the children—hungry, thirsty, helplessly clinging to their parents with fear in their eyes.

Occasionally, we would find lost or abandoned horses, but even they were parched, and too weak to take us far. There were no trains running. Only an occasional military truck or tank convoy would pass—and none offered us a ride. I don't remember eating anything during that walk. We would stop periodically when we came to a small river or creek to drink water, but in the dry pit of summer, these were often muddy, insect-ridden pools more likely to make us sick than quench our thirst. The hours dragged painfully. All we could think about was food—which only made us hungrier. Worse, our cigarette supply ran so low we had to share one cigarette at a time to stave off hunger.

We passed fields and small villages, looking for any sign of a collective farm. Nearly a week into our walk, we overheard people talking about a mineral spring not far from where we were. This didn't sound like a long-term solution, but we desperately needed a break to hydrate and assess our plans. The springs were a few kilometers off the road, through a field. Most people, especially those with heavy carts, preferred to remain on the road, progressing toward their destinations. But we had no encumbrances, and any excuse to get out of the hot sun was welcome.

Those last kilometers passed agonizingly slowly. Searching the horizon for any sign of a mineral spring, we made out trees in the distance, across the field, and hoped this would bring us closer to fresh water. Willing our aching limbs, we lumbered across the field, ignoring the sores and blisters on our feet. Entering the woods, we scoured the area, listening and looking for any sign of a spring. It was Bider who spotted it first. "Hallelujah!" he cried, pointing to a rocky ridge with a flowing spring and pools.

The spring was a haven. Dozens of other refugees, gaunt and aching, bathed in the refreshing water. People came and went, but we stayed at the springs for a few days, trying to recover from the journey. Our feet were blistered and bloody. I think we had survived on adrenaline and cigarettes. We immersed ourselves in cool water, wincing from our stinging sores. Gulping mouthfuls of the clear water, we slowly became giddy—the endorphins overtaking our bodies—elated that we managed to find this refuge. The last meal we'd had was in Rostov, and with our bellies sloshing with water, we searched for food.

Not far from the springs were some berry bushes and fruit trees. I remember filling my stomach with fruit until I became nauseous. We spent the next few days bathing and tending to our battered feet, eating fruit, and sleeping under the stars. We would constantly discuss our options, debating the pros and cons of each. What if the Germans would take over, where would we go? Was there anything we could do for our families? Would the Soviet Union protect us, or were we in just as much danger with the Russians?

We spoke with as many of the other fleeing refugees as possible. Most were headed south, but some went north and east toward the Caspian Sea. Everyone stayed away from the Black Sea; the risk of falling into German hands was too high.

Most of the people we encountered at the spring were foreign refugees like us. We asked each person we met if they knew of a collective farm, and everyone answered the same: Yes, there are a few in the region, but I don't know where they are. A lot of good that did us. The other recurring theme was that the Germans were coming. We couldn't stay any longer at our watering hole. We decided that we would just return to the main road and soldier on across the countryside to look for a collective farm that could absorb us.

It was our luck that later that day a lone young man with a thick foreign accent appeared. He was from somewhere in the southern Caucasus and was on his way north to check in on relatives. Pircus—highly skeptical by this point that we'd ever find a collective farm—sarcastically asked, "You don't happen to work on a kolkhoz, do you?" To our collective shock, the young man said yes. Somewhat surprised at the question, the young man studied us. "I've been travelling for more than a week from the farm where I work," he said. "It's outside Grozny, called Kalinovka."

We all sat up attentively, offering the man some of the fruit we'd collected, eager to hear more. In between grateful mouthfuls of fruit, he proceeded to tell us about his kolkhoz. "Kalinovka is fairly peaceful, despite some of the Chechen resistance near Grozny," he said. "They will soon be preparing for the fall harvest and would likely welcome able young men to help work; they would offer food and shelter. I hope to make it back in time, but I need to check on relatives in Krasnodar Krai."

The young man looked off into the distance. "There are a lot of people on the road," he observed. "The farm may not have the capacity to absorb all those who need help. There are other farms near Krasnodar Krai and near Grozny, but I don't know anyone there." After he finished gulping down some cool water, he stood to go. "I want to try and reach my relatives before nightfall," he said. "Good luck."

"One more thing," I asked, smiling. "What is your name?"

"Aslan," he replied, returning the smile. "Ask for Oleg when you get there. Let him know I am near my relatives' village." I promised I would, and he walked off into the afternoon light. With some idea at least of where we were going, we all went to sleep that night feeling optimistic.

We rose early the next morning, still aching from the sores on our feet, but in much better condition than when we arrived. Leaving our oasis behind, we set off toward Kalinovka. Our stomachs rumbled from the fruit, and we all suffered from diarrhea. We finally had a destination, but the road was no less grueling for that. Hours on end, we trudged with battered feet and tattered clothes. The road was choked with masses of people, heaving along their belongings, homeless and in despair. We walked all day and collapsed at night, sleeping by the side of the dirt road. Once, we found a few weak horses that we rode for a day, but without enough food and water, they gave out on us.

Several days into this endless march toward Kalinovka, we began to consider seriously the possibility we might die somewhere along this road. Our morale—fairly high as we left Rostov and later renewed at the mineral spring—sank toward despair. As our energy ebbed away, conversation tapered off into silence. Our thoughts drifted inward. I constantly thought about my family. I feared for their safety and felt helpless. Maybe it was a mistake to leave? What if I had stayed? Maybe we could have found a place to hide together in nearby villages? Did they resent me for leaving? Who was to say that I was better off clutching my leather coat in the middle of a wasteland in the summer heat? Of course, there was no way I could have known at the time what was happening in Dubno and across the rest of Europe, but the guilt and regret wore on me terribly, making the journey all the more painful.

I was delirious by the time we arrived. I vaguely recall only that there was a small band of us propping one another up as a rush of people came to splash water on us. Somehow, we'd made it to Kalinovka. All of us: Bider, Groinim, Pircus, Itzchik, Jake, and me.

Chapter 9:
Collective Farm

I don't remember how long I slept or even how I got there, but at some point I woke up in a barn, covered in straw. The summer air was thick and humid, and people were being called to a meeting. We gathered in the courtyard outside the empty dining hall. Dozens of refugees of various ethnic backgrounds—including a few Jews with their own harrowing tales of escape—milled about quietly waiting for the farm director to make his announcement.

Waiting for the meeting to start, I got my first good look around. Kalinovka was a sprawling farm with poorly maintained machinery and agricultural supplies. The farm had lost many of its young men to military conscription, and the few hands that remained to work the fields needed more help to keep up with the national demand for food. It turned out that an influx of desperate refugees provided a short-term solution to their problems. There were a good number of women—hair pulled back by head coverings, sleeves rolled up showing sinewy arms—who looked like they toiled in the fields. Looking off to the horizon, I felt as though I was in the middle of nowhere. There were fields as far as the eye could see and rolling hills off in the distance.

Eventually, a short, balding, sweaty man emerged, wiping his spectacles with a dirty handkerchief. Pircus and I exchanged a smile as he introduced himself as Oleg, the farm director. Reading from a sheet of paper handed him by his attentive assistant, Oleg recited Stalin's proclamations and hailed the greatness of the USSR. Apparently a deeply patriotic Communist Party member, Oleg raged against the German invasion. Following a lengthy speech of routine indoctrination, Oleg folded away the paper and spoke plainly with the band of refugees. He explained that the harvest would be gathered soon and that all workers would contribute to the effort. The highest priority would be to provide food for soldiers fighting on the front lines; the remainder would be left for the workers. Oleg promised us food and shelter in exchange for our work. Given the hell we'd been through, a stable place to sleep and food to eat sounded wonderful. The joy didn't last long.

Several seasoned farm hands hovered near the dining hall entrance, twisting toothpicks between their teeth and sizing up the slovenly group of refugees before them. Two young ladies eased up chairs behind wooden tables and pulled out thick ledgers. The farm director requested that the refugees form a line to be registered. Once the ladies had entered all of the names into their ledgers, they assigned each person to a group led by one of the farmhands. We were sorted into small groups and assigned living quarters.

The conditions were terrible—dilapidated barns, their dirt floors strewn with hay and rotting grass. Beds were coarse burlap tarps or sacks positioned haphazardly on piles of straw. All of the barn doors were left open to ventilate the stench of dirty sweat and mildew that permeated the air.

We milled about that afternoon, listening to the stories of other refugees, empathizing with the hollow look in their eyes. Kalinovka was cramped with displaced people from across the region. The dirty quarters—coupled with a lack of sanitary facilities—bred lice infestations throughout the collective farm. Kalinovka was bordered by the River Terek, which served as the only bathing site. Most young men elected to shave their heads just to avoid the lice. I didn't want to shave my head. I had a thick head of wavy hair and hoped to keep it that way. With the waning light, we eased ourselves toward our sleeping quarters, exhausted but relieved to be free of bombardments and running. As the moonlight swept across the farm and wolves howled in the distance, I covered my face with my leather coat and fell asleep.

The first summer at Kalinovka passed quickly. There was always something to be done. We woke early and worked late: tending to crops, cleaning and repairing facilities and equipment. It was monotonous work, but not too difficult. Food was minimal—bare subsistence rations of bread, potatoes, and occasional fruit.

Curious about other members of the collective, I would speak with people from various backgrounds during cigarette breaks. Somehow, in our broken Russian, we managed to communicate. Eventually, these relationships led to the development of a black market via which we traded amongst ourselves for, say, extra cigarettes, a hat or shirt, or, if lucky, some wine or vodka. As the summer waned, the workload increased. We collected thousands of bushels of grain, which were processed into flour and packaged for shipment.

The months were peaceful but emotionally grinding. Here we were, seemingly safe from violent conflict, yet unable to receive word about the fate of our families. I worried every day about my parents, my siblings, my friends. The thought of my brother begging me to take him haunted me. Rarely a night went by without someone in the barn screaming from night terrors.

Life at Kalinovka became routine and depressing. The workers gathered the harvest, yet barely had enough to eat. Whatever was harvested went straight to the Russian army. As winter approached and harvest season ended, people mostly sat around in the little collective village, listened to the radio for news, and rationed food as carefully as possible so as not to starve during the colder months.

Food shortages caused bitter conflict. I had taken to hiding one piece of bread in my haystack, just in case I would not receive a portion the next day. One early winter afternoon, I went to replace my emergency bread, when I noticed it was missing. I started shouting at the top of my lungs, my anger and hunger propelling me beyond reason. A Russian who bunked next to me snapped back at me to calm down. That was all the provocation needed to push me completely over the edge. I accused the Russian of stealing it. The Russian denied it. I charged, tackling him to the ground. We fought with wild abandon as hands pulled at us from all sides trying to separate us. The Russian spat curses at me as I vowed revenge.

With our brawl escalating, Groinim—speaking in Yiddish—pleaded with me to calm down. After a few moments, we were pulled apart, patting the blood from our lips with our sleeves. We were both panting and fuming. Groinim finally seized my attention. With a guilty look, he implored me to forgive him. He explained that *he* had taken the bread while I was out because he was too ill to leave the barn. He apologized repeatedly. I patted him on the shoulder and slunk over to the Russian. Not having understood a thing that Groinim said, the Russian glared at me. Even though it was the right thing to do, I hated apologizing to him. I told him that I shouldn't have jumped to conclusions and accused him. Reluctantly accepting the apology, he grabbed his hat and nodded. Storming out, he spat on the dirt, and under his breath he grunted an irritated, "Yid!" I ignored the insult, turned to look at my friends, and then we all broke out in laughter.

Winter, 1941, was the first winter I spent away from Dubno. The months were long and dismal—food was scarce, work was robotic, and war, it seemed, would never end. Often, there was nothing to do during the winter months other than find a way to stay warm. Boredom and hunger often led to confrontation. There were near-daily skirmishes over trivial issues.

One gloomy morning, I was exhausted from working the day before on an empty stomach and needed to sleep. Sergey, an ogre of a supervisor, would routinely bark at the refugees, telling them they were lucky to have a place to eat and sleep. He never missed an opportunity to harass someone, and would often use the butt of his rifle to ensure that orders were followed. This particular morning, Sergey stomped into my quarters looking for people to comb the fields for traces of wheat. The fields were covered in frost, making this task utterly pointless. That didn't stop Sergey. He was shouting—at everyone and no one in particular. I hoped that if I just lay still he would continue his tirade elsewhere and calm down after a few shots of vodka. No such luck.

"Get up!" Sergey screamed, looming over me. Before I could explain that I'd worked an extremely long day and didn't have the energy to get up, he was kicking my feet sternly with his boots and shouting again. I was shocked. I sat up and glared at him. In an instant, he had spun his rifle around and was pointing the muzzle right at me. Instinctively, I sprang to my feet and snatched the rifle right out of his hands.

Sergey looked as stunned as I felt. Neither one of us expected it, but there I was with the gun in my hand. The look in Sergey's eyes changed from shock to fear. I managed to collect myself, hoping that my shaking hands didn't give away my nervousness. I looked at Sergey squarely and said, "Leave me alone." I handed him the rifle, which he accepted meekly, nodding his head. Looking like he had no idea what hit him, Sergey dragged himself out of the barn. I dropped down into my straw bed trembling with adrenaline.

Part of me worried that Sergey would seek revenge, but I never felt that he would actually kill anyone. Sometimes bullies need someone to stand up to them. After hearing my story about my confrontation with Sergey, Jake suggested I avoid him for a while. Leaving for somewhere else sounded like a great idea. The barren winter had left many without sufficient sustenance and several people starved to death. Bider and Itzchik had left Kalinovka on official orders to go help with collecting supplies. Jake, Groinim, Pircus, and I had grown thin and desperate for food. Although Kalinovka provided us a refuge from frontline conflict, it was in effect a starvation camp, and we worried that we wouldn't survive the winter on our paltry rations. Pircus suggested that we chance a hike to Grozny, where we might be able to barter for food. No one had a better idea—and it would get me away from Sergey—so we agreed to do it.

We scoured the grounds for anything of value, pooled together our possessions, and displayed our wares across a burlap mat. It was a sad collection of trinkets: a rusty can opener; dull cutlery; torn and dirty fabric. Sitting around by candlelight, we discussed our plan. Our trek would take us through the Black Hills, over paths rumored to be menaced by lurking bandits and criminals. Worse yet, Chechnya was in the middle of an insurgency against the Soviet Union. We risked death by militia, Soviet retaliation, or criminals. It was an 80-kilometer roundtrip hike over steep terrain in the dead of winter. Then again, we were starving to death. The dormant fields left only maintenance work to be done around the farm. We figured we could likely disappear for a couple days without anyone noticing.

We rose early the next morning and made our way toward the Black Hills in the pre-dawn chill. Walking across the plains as the sun broke over the horizon, I felt a peacefulness—as if we were just a group of friends heading out for a morning hike, not starving refugees desperate for food to survive. There was beauty in the sound of gurgling streams, chirping birds, and the rustling of crunchy leaves tickled by a gentle breeze.

As we started our ascent, the sun beamed brightly, piercing the web of barren tree branches. As we climbed higher, we were enveloped by a dull, pale mist that hid the sun, the sky, and the beauty of the forest below. The white cloud grew so thick that we could not see more than a couple meters ahead. Ghostly trees would appear and disappear as we passed. If we strayed just far enough apart, we could make out only our silhouettes, advancing silently into the white emptiness.

It was afternoon by the time we arrived at Grozny under an overcast sky that seemed to follow us from the timberline. We were exhausted. We stopped only to drink from the narrow, flowing creeks to hydrate and to help wash down our crusts of stale, black bread. Grozny appeared shrouded in despair but safe from the insurgency— at least for a while. *Babushkas* tottered on cobbled streets, muttering about their absent sons. Young teen boys in weathered clothes shared cigarettes, each taking a deep drag, holding in the smoke for longer than usual to savor the taste and allay the hunger in their empty bellies. Storefronts were empty. Eventually, we came upon a makeshift market where goods were traded.

We each fished out our sad collection of junk, polishing and cleaning the objects with the hem of our shirts to make them more appealing. The challenge was finding something to eat now and something to trade at Kalinovka later. We managed to secure a needle and thread, so we could patch our clothes. To satisfy our immediate hunger, we acquired fresh bread and some preserved jam, which had the added benefit of the glass container that we could use or trade later. The best trade was fabric for a pail of honey — golden brown, smooth and sticky.

We were tempted to dip our bread in the honey, letting its viscous sweetness ooze over our tongues, but we knew we needed to save this delicacy for later; this was our only gold to trade for food. We stood around the pail for a moment, staring at the opaque glitter, mesmerized by its richness, inviting us to dive in head first, satiating our souls. "One finger?" suggested Pircus with a childish grin. We each dipped into the honey, coating our finger, twirling our hand so the excess wrapped around itself while raising our candied hand to our mouths. Giddy, we savored our treat, wandering toward the city's outskirts to find a place to sleep for the night.

It didn't take long before we came upon an abandoned barn, the livestock that once occupied it long gone. We divided the bread and jam, saving half for the journey back. We then fell ravenously on our allotted portions, relieving our grumbling stomachs, and quickly fell asleep, buried in the hay.

Lumbering back to Kalinovka the next morning with our added weight of honey was a welcome burden; in a time of war, we were rich! We fantasized about all the food we would receive for a glass of honey; we dreamed about smoked fish and meat, pickled vegetables, thick slices of cheese, and hot stew simmering in an oily broth. We forgot about the potential danger from the woods, the threat that our honey might be stolen—until we heard a call across a thicket of bushes.

We froze, like exposed deer caught at a riverbed. It was a human voice, but murmuring incomprehensible sounds. We edged forward along the misty morning hillside, acutely aware of our every step and sound. In the clearing around the thicket was a man kneeling on a mat, prostrating as he mumbled—oblivious to our presence in the distance. I had never met a Muslim before and was only vaguely aware of Islam, so I was unfamiliar with his custom. As long as he didn't bother us, we wouldn't bother him. Cautiously, we continued onward, the faint mumbling fading behind us.

The last rays of sunlight arched into the sky as we approached the barren fields of Kalinovka. Carefully concealing the pail of honey under a tarp of weathered clothes, we made it safely back to our quarters, where we collapsed on our beds.

I woke lazily, stiff from the exertion of the past two days. Eventually, I gingerly walked on my aching feet to collect my paltry breakfast of watery potato soup, made bearable only by some extra salt. A new shipment of supplies arrived to prepare the farm for spring planting—meaning that a fresh supply of food would likely be among the packaged boxes. Approaching a group of farm officials smoking near the supply trucks, I asked for a match and joined them for a cigarette. My Russian was slowly improving, and I had developed a degree of trust with a couple of the younger managers. Volunteering to help unload a couple boxes with a young man named Slava, I had the opportunity to explore trading some of the honey.

The thought of honey made Slava's mouth water, his eyes darting over the sealed boxes. Slava offered a loaf of bread for a glass of honey, to which I readily agreed. He provided me with an empty jar, and we agreed to meet later that night by the mill. Criminals in the night, we swapped our goods, each equally delighted. Groinim, Pircus, and I were each able to trade a glass for food, which we all shared. That trip to Grozny looked like it had been worth the risk. For a few small glasses of honey, we had collected enough food to help us survive a couple weeks. Sitting around chewing our black-market bread, Pircus was smiling, clearly pleased with himself.

"Nu, Pircus, what's so funny?" Jake asked.

Pircus wanted to keep us in suspense but couldn't resist any longer. "I met a couple Polish girls!" he blurted out with a toothy smile. We all leaned in to hear more. "I was looking for someone to trade honey, and they said that they have wine to share if we have some extra food."

Pircus was getting excited now. "They are coming over tonight!" he exclaimed, giggling like a schoolboy. He went on to describe how one had beautiful green eyes and the other long blonde hair. By now, he had us all wound up as well. We each started asking about them and their friends. It had been a long time since any of us had the attention of a pretty young girl, and despite our miserable circumstances, our desire was undiminished. We were all talking over one another, excited about spending time with these girls. We collected the food that we were willing to share and straightened up the barn for our visitors. I went out to collect some firewood. We even braved the freezing cold to clean ourselves up as best we could; you never knew how the night might go! Elated to have a party, we forgot about our environment.

Shortly after dark, as promised, a small group of Polish girls arrived, with bottles of wine tucked under their overcoats. We didn't care that they were rail thin; in the flickering light of the fire, and flattered by our imaginations, these girls were gorgeous, with flowing locks of golden curls and ruby lips. Pircus stood to welcome them in, and when he exchanged a kiss on the cheek with one of the girls, our hormones completely overcame our senses.

We drank so much that I can't even remember any of the girls' names. It didn't take much to get us drunk; we hardly had enough calories in us to keep us alive. We began by toasting with the wine, which loosened us all up. Jake, feeling the mood, had his eye on one girl and went to his stash to produce a bottle of vodka. He offered her the first shot, and then shared with us all. Pircus and I performed songs and dances to the amusement of our small audience.

In a moment of revelry, Pircus placed his finger over his lips to quiet us down to share a secret as he giggled, drunk. He then crept over to his quarters, removed some wood, and produced the pail of honey. As we stared at the riches in his hands, the girls ooohed and aaahed, each one squeezing us more closely, giggling. Pircus spread thin layers of honey over bread and passed the delicacy around like a benevolent king. The rest of the night became a blur. I remember feeling wonderful—happily drunk, savoring tasty food, basking in the camaraderie of my friends and the uplifting warmth of a pretty girl in my arms. At some point in the night, I passed out in the hay, smiling.

The happiness all came crashing down the next morning when I woke up to Groinim shouting curses and kicking everything he saw. My head was pounding, and it took me a few moments to register what he was saying. The barn was a disaster; I couldn't tell if it was from the night before or from Groinim's hysterics. "It's gone! It's gone!" he kept shouting. "Damn it, damn it, damn it!"

I looked around and tried to focus. Pircus had his head in his hands. The others were waking up just as groggy and confused. Suddenly, Groinim's words sank in: The girls and the pail of honey were gone.

PART 2 – SOLDIER

Chapter 10:
Defend Crimea

Perpetually hungry, we dragged our way through the final weeks of winter, eagerly anticipating warmer spring weather and the prospect of food. The limited news reports were terrible: Germany was expanding its offensive, and the nightmarish prospect of a global Nazi empire was becoming all too real.

On a mild morning, a small military convoy arrived at Kalinovka. A weathered commander pulled himself out of his jeep and had the farm director gather all of the laborers for a meeting. Young Soviet soldiers sat on the backs of trucks, hollow-eyed and exhausted. The commander informed us that the German army had advanced toward Krasnodar and was making its way toward Orginikidze. A rush of panicked conversation immediately spread among the farm hands and refugees. The commander eventually regained our attention and explained that he had orders to select all able-bodied men to serve and defend the Soviet Union from the German advance. The commander said that Marshal Budenny was leading a North Caucasus Front to resist the German advance into the Caucasus. He had received these orders from the central military command and came from Naur to Kalinovka and other collective farms in the region to conscript as many soldiers as possible. Those selected would depart the following morning.

We were dumbfounded by the news. No one had military training. Most of the people on the farm had never fired a gun before. A small murmur broke the initial silence following the commander's remarks. Quietly, the non-Russian refugees protested, saying that they didn't want to die on the front. Like us, these people—Jew and non-Jew alike—felt that they had fled their homes to escape war. They were not soldiers. What good could they do in the fight against the Germans? These quieter voices were drowned out by the angrier ones. Some of the refugees argued that we had no choice but to fight. Germany had caused this war, and fighting back was the only alternative for our survival.

The Soviet military officials largely ignored the opinions of the refugees. For them, this wasn't an issue up for discussion. This was not a democracy. We were going to serve whether we liked it or not. As we bickered among ourselves, a sharp whistle stopped our conversation abruptly. The commander and a lieutenant ordered all men to form a line. Looking back on it now, it was an awfully sad group of young men—weathered, tired, hungry, and weak. The lieutenant paced down the line of refugees, selecting with a tap on the shoulder anyone that was not ill or injured—about 40 of us. They may as well have picked everyone. After this short process, all that remained were a few obviously injured people, a few longtime farmhands, and women.

The commander then stepped on a crate and addressed the new conscripts. He started slowly, gradually building his speech like a symphony. The words rose rhythmically, incrementally instilling confidence in us all. He made a special effort to recognize us by publicly praising our value, attempting to make each of us feel that our individual effort would be the factor to turn the tide of the war. He inspired us to join a cause greater than ourselves—an apocalyptic battle of good versus evil. He was a gifted speaker, and even though the choice to enlist had not been ours, he was effectively recruiting us.

I remember the looks in the eyes of these boys, listening to the commander speak. They were mesmerized. It didn't take long for the group of new conscripts to start to believe. The commander noticed the change. On cue, he ordered us to attention. We all snapped into our best posture, squaring our shoulders, puffing out our chests, clicking our heels together. Then, in a grave tone, he pledged us to an oath to defend the Soviet Union. He spoke deliberately, emphasizing each word. We repeated these words in broken Russian and foreign accents. The commander looked at us with pride. We could feel it. We now had a purpose. Upon the conclusion of our oath, the commander paused theatrically to scan the faces of his new recruits and shouted, "*Pobeda!* (Victory to the Soviet Union!)" In answer, we erupted in cheers.

Those staying behind came to thank us and wish us well. We soon dispersed to meet with a sergeant who welcomed us to the army. We would be issued uniforms later, but we were each immediately supplied with a PPSh-41 submachine gun and some very basic instruction on how to operate it. Then each of us was handed half a bottle of wine and some bread. We drank and ate and shared stories with our fellow soldiers.

Jake and I laughed about being soldiers. Neither of us were remotely qualified for combat, but we figured that at least in the army we would receive some basic provisions—which was better than starving to death on a collective farm. At some level, of course, I was aware of the risk to life and limb that came with being a soldier, but given all I'd been through since fleeing my home the summer before, there was some comfort in having a gun to defend myself and joining the fight against the bastards that had stolen my life in Dubno. This was all still an adventure to me, so I didn't dwell on the dangers. And besides, I didn't have a choice.

We all woke the next morning with hangovers. The dawn light revealed empty bottles of wine and vodka strewn about the smoldering embers of our campfire, reminding us of the revelry of the night before. I ran my hand through my matted hair and rubbed my face to massage away the headache. Groggy, I slowly rose and stretched, finally noticing the beauty of the spring morning. The scent of crisp dew wafted in the fresh clean air, reminding me of spring in Dubno.

Peter, our unit commander, approached us, passing out cigarettes to allay the morning hunger. A young man in his early 20s, Peter was roughly our age. He was a typical blond-haired, blue-eyed

Russian, flashing the gold-capped teeth that were so popular at the time. It was clear he wanted to develop some rapport with us through the drinks and smokes—slapping us on the shoulders as if we were old friends reuniting after a long absence. He told a few dirty jokes, which helped to quell some of the anxiety we felt about what was to come next.

Peter then directed us to sit together as a group. He informed us that we now had our first orders: defend Crimea. While in Kalinovka, we had learned that from August to November 1941, the Germans had captured Dnepropetrovsk, Kiev, Kharkhiv, and Rostov. The Soviets later reclaimed Rostov. With the Red Army emboldened by its success in ejecting the Germans from Rostov, we were to be sent to Kerch to defend Crimea from the German advance.

Peter told us that he did not have any uniforms or military supplies other than the PPSh submachine guns, which were provided. He said that later that afternoon we were to board a train for Crimea, where we would report to a base camp to receive further instructions and supplies. In the meantime, he divided us into small groups for training in how to use the PPSh.

We were all so awkward with our new automatic weapons. This was the first time I'd ever held a gun of any kind, so I was apprehensive at first. We learned the fundamentals of how the PPSh operated, how to keep it clean, and basic safety guidelines. We then fired off a few precious rounds for practice. Nearly every one of us lost control of the gun the first time we fired it, unprepared for the force of the blast. After a few hours, I became more comfortable with the gun, learning enough to feel confident I'd know how to use it if needed. It was empowering. Even though German conquest seemed inevitable, it felt good to know that I would be able to defend myself if I had to.

By the time the sun dipped behind the trees, Peter was calling for all of the soldiers to gather and board the train. In his typical, confident style, he stood at the edge of the coach car, holding on to the handle, allowing the edges of his boots to hang over the doorway. "*Ribyata, lads!*" he called out. "Now is your chance for revenge! Those bastard Germans killed our families! We go to Crimea, and we will force the Germans back to Berlin or kill every last one of them!"

The motivational speech appeared to work. Peter was easy to like. He made it seem possible that a group of gaunt refugees in shabby civilian clothes could drive back German guns and tanks. Peter marshaled us onto the train and started singing patriotic Russian songs. As we left Kalinovka behind, a raucous chorus of songs carried us into the evening to defend Crimea.

The trip toward Crimea was largely peaceful, soothed by the rhythmic roll on the track. A couple days filled with stretches of sleep, cigarette breaks, and whispered conversations. Even though we were heading into certain danger, no one was chasing us, no bombs and bullets were exploding around us. We passed breadbasket fields, deserted farmhouses, and fires that burned on the horizon.

Peter sat next to me and said, "Wolf isn't Russian. You'll want to have a strong Russian name." Searching Peter's face, I could see that he was trying to protect me from anti-Semitism within the Soviet ranks. "What is your father's name?" Peter quietly asked in a friendly tone. "Nussen," I responded, immediately drifting in thought toward home. Peter paused for a moment, and then with a gleam in his eye, whispered, "Vladimir Nusseyonovich. Now that is a strong Russian name." He smiled, patted me on the shoulder, and then left to speak with other soldiers. It seemed settled; I was now Vladimir.

Eventually, the train slowed through a small town crossing. The train swayed, leaning heavily toward one side, then back to the other, as it proceeded cautiously along the crossing. We pressed our faces to the windows, eager to see the condition of the town. It was getting dark, but there was still enough daylight to see the streets and structures near the train; everything further off was blurred in gray dusk shadows. The streets were largely empty except for the odd bundles left behind in a hasty evacuation: carts, clothes, pots, broken plates. It was an eerie feeling, passing through this ghost town, as if the entire population had mysteriously disappeared. I don't remember what city this was, but I'll never forget what happened next.

As the train pulled out of town and around a bend to the left, the cars swayed sharply to the right, pressing us against the right side of the train and forcing our gaze out into the darkening landscape. We heard a rumble, as if the ground were shaking. It was difficult to make out initially. No one said a word. We peered out into the emptiness, trying to identify what caused the sound. The rumble grew louder, like rolling thunder during a summer storm.

We heard voices, the shouts of men, partially drowned out by the now roaring sound. Then we noticed it. Hundreds of horses and trucks were racing in the opposite direction. Judging by the now deafening volume of the sound, only a small fraction of the total number of horses and trucks were visible. Before the panic set in, we heard Russian voices calling out, so at least we knew that the mass of people were not Germans attacking. We started talking over one another, trying to figure out what was going on.

A senior officer on horseback slowed near our train, close enough for us to shout and get his attention. He noticed our guns and rode up to us asking who we were and where we were going. A few of the men shouted back confidently that we were newly enlisted soldiers with orders to defend Crimea. Incredulous, the officer grabbed his head and roared, "Kerch was already captured by the Germans!" Pointing in the direction we were heading, he shouted, "They are right there!" The officer kicked his horse and sped away. The reality took a moment to sink in: These soldiers were retreating, and we were heading directly into German hands.

This caused total panic throughout the train. Everyone talked over one another, but no one knew what to do. The train started to speed up, racing into the void ahead. Should we jump off of the train now? What if the officer was wrong? Should we notify the conductor? The train continued to charge, leaving the rumbling retreat further behind us, bringing impending danger closer with each churn of the wheels. We were all standing around, fidgeting nervously, uncertain what to do. Suddenly, the train cars jolted in succession as the brakes screeched, causing everyone standing to tumble over.

Save for a distant glow of burning cities, it was pitch black outside. No one moved or said a word. The silence enveloped everything around us and time stood still. I looked around at all of the nervous faces, darting their eyes and shifting uncomfortably in their seats. Peter was just about to say something, rising from his seat slowly to face us. It was at that moment that the blast of a tremendous explosion sent shockwaves throughout the train, rattling everything. Peter wrapped his arms over his head and tumbled over onto the floor of the car. The coach car shook violently, jolting us from our seats. The train was being bombarded by Germans.

Chaos ensued. It was impossible to tell one person from another. A mass of limbs clawed to get out. Another crash, this one closer than the first, shattered windows, casting shards of glass everywhere. I scrambled toward the rear of the car, covering my head and looking for an exit. Crawling to the vestibule of the car, I pulled myself up using the wrought iron rails. There was no time to think. The train wasn't safe, and it was impossible to know what dangers lay ahead of me in the vast darkness.

Clutching my gun, I jumped off the train onto the rocky earth and crouched down immediately, imagining bullets and shells incoming any minute. The other soldiers fled the train similarly, wildly running into the black fields. Several of us managed to find one another as we ran. I faintly recall hearing Peter's voice shouting that we should run toward Salsk, where we would be armed and protected. In the madness of the moment, I had no idea where Salsk was or how to get there. I knew that I had to get as far away from the train—and Crimea—as possible.

Another crash and the train rattled off the tracks. The sound of exploding mortars neared, closing in on our location. I imagined the German tanks and infantry fanning across the plain, preparing to pounce on us at any moment. I shuddered at the thought of capture. I pulled myself together and started running. I called out for Jake as I sprinted away from the train. Each burst of mortar fire drowned out my shouts, but I kept screaming his name. After a minute or so, I heard his voice echoing my calls. "Wolf! Wolf!" he shouted, running somewhere nearby in the darkness. Finally linking up, we pushed each other to run faster.

There were hundreds of us that fled the train. There may have been thousands stranded on it. I never stopped to look back, hoping that each step I took would bring me closer to safety. I ran to the point of exhaustion, leaving my aching body no alternative but to walk. As soon as I could catch my breath, we would run again. I lost track of how many of my Kalinovka refugee-soldiers were with me. The night was a blur. We plodded on foot until the sound of the thundering bombs faded. It was early dawn by the time we finally felt free of imminent threat.

With the sunrise piercing the horizon, we stopped to survey our surroundings. We didn't stray too far from the train tracks, in the hope of eventually finding a train headed east. But otherwise it was impossible to tell where we were. All around was vast countryside, dotted by burning fires in the distance.

Jake and I exchanged looks of utter frustration. I couldn't believe it. Here I was again: repeating the same escape I'd endured roughly nine months earlier. I felt hunted again, a refugee again. This war was no longer a game, no longer exciting. I was tired, angry, and worried for my family. Feeling the PPSh in my hand, I told myself, *No, I am not the same refugee as before—I am a soldier.*

As the sky brightened, we came upon a small farm and noticed workers loading supplies and bags into the cargo bay of a truck. We immediately set off in a sprint, hoping to reach them before they could drive off. Panting, we approached the men, who were visibly shocked by the sight of us—exhausted, dirty civilians with machine guns. I explained who we were and told them about the bombing outside Kerch. Their eyes widened in alarm at the advancing German threat, and they quickened their packing. They said they were heading toward Krasnodar and invited us to ride in the cargo bay.

We collapsed on overstuffed burlap bags. There must have been about a dozen of us, some from Kalinovka, others who managed to escape the bombing in Crimea. By now we were all on high alert, aware that at any moment the truck could also be attacked. But we had little choice. The only way to get away from the German advance was to ride further southeast.

Despite our exhaustion, we argued about what to do next. We had no command. We did not know exactly where we were. We didn't even know where we should go. There were a few soldiers in uniform who'd managed to escape the bombing on the train. They were confident that we would find a command in Krasnodar that would give us directions. Those of us in civilian clothes had no reason to doubt them. So, it seemed settled: Report to an officer in Krasnodar and inform him about the bombing outside Crimea.

The truck rumbled on for most of the day, arriving in Krasnodar by late afternoon. Smoke filled the air. Large segments of the city were abandoned, left to burn. We thanked the men for the ride, hopping off at an industrial area outside the city center. Wandering around the streets, we covered our mouths with rags from our clothes to limit the amount of smoke we inhaled. It didn't help. We coughed incessantly. There was no apparent Russian military presence.

We wandered aimlessly in the smoke, looking for any signs of Soviet military. "*Durak*, idiot," mumbled one Russian refugees under his breath.

"Where is the base camp?" demanded another. It wasn't the soldiers' fault. They'd thought the military would be there. And perhaps they were somewhere, but it was impossible to find them—especially in the thickening smoke.

The insults continued until the soldiers had had enough. They started shouting at the refugees: *How the hell were we supposed to know where the military were?* Tempers rose on both sides, fueled by fatigue, frustration, and stress.

We went to Krasnodar based on your advice, the refugees complained.

Where else were we supposed to go? the soldiers retorted.

The comments grew increasingly accusatory, instigating a shoving match, which quickly escalated to a fistfight. Then, the worst happened. The soldiers drew their weapons and loaded them. The refugees did the same. With the Germans bearing down on us, here we stood: refugees and soldiers drawing weapons on one another.

Jake and I kept our hands on our guns, but we were not in the middle of the fight. The soldiers and refugees were now screaming at each other. Trying to quell the tension, one of the refugees fired a round into the sky, the crackle of the shot reverberating through the buildings. We were lucky that we didn't all kill each other right then and there. Instead, everyone froze. We all looked at the refugee who'd fired the shot. The soldiers immediately reprimanded him: *What if there are Germans here? Now you've given away our position!*

The refugee stood there stupidly, unable to respond. For better or worse, this stopped the argument, but it increased the stress. The soldiers spat—*the hell with you all*—and ran off together. Jake and I wanted no further part of these crazy people, so we ran in another direction, leaving the other refugees arguing among themselves about what to do.

Jake and I agreed on going back to Kalinovka. It was the only place we knew where we were somewhat confident we'd be safe. The journey to Kalinovka was as long and tiresome as the first time we did it. This time, at least, there were more trucks traveling south toward Chechnya, making the journey easier on our feet. The PPSh was really helpful; it was only the guns that marked us as soldiers and not just two among millions of starving refugees. We didn't receive much help, but whatever bits of small rations we received along the way helped us stay alive.

I was lucky to have left Krasnodar when I did. If I had ended up stranded there or swept up in some Soviet command near Krasnodar, I may not have survived the war. In mid-August 1942, just months after Jake and I fled Krasnodar, the Germans occupied the city. They controlled the area until February 1943. In the intervening months, the Germans killed hundreds of Jews.[xi]

It was late afternoon when we stumbled into the courtyard at Kalinovka. A small group of farmhands and Russian soldiers were crouched over their tables talking and smoking. Once they noticed who we were, they sprang from their seats and offered us their places. A few girls rushed to get us some bread and water, slapping both down on the table. They were all collectively stunned to see us and peppered us with questions. In between grateful bites of hard bread, we recounted the news about Crimea, the bombing of the train, and Krasnodar. The soldiers eagerly asked about Peter; we didn't know what had happened to him. Amid wild speculation about the German advance, some advocated fleeing further east and south, while others urged fighting the Germans to the death. This discussion continued well into the night, but I was too exhausted to participate. Hobbling over to my place in the old barn, I collapsed on the burlap mat and slept.

I woke early the next morning. Despite my aching muscles, I felt better after the night's rest. I looked at my dirty hands and ripped clothes. I smelled awful. I walked over to the river and found a girl doing laundry. She offered me some soap so that I could wash myself and my clothes. I plunged my head into the cool, refreshing, spring-fed water, letting the current peel away the soot from my hair.

I scrubbed until I started to feel numb from the cold water.

Shivering my way out of the river, I shook and wiped the water off of me, sitting in the morning sun to dry off. It was difficult to believe that this was my life. I struggled to comprehend how I'd ended up in this situation and, more importantly, how I would find my way out of it. The enormity of the war, its effects on me and on everything around me, was too much to wrap my head around. I shook my hands through my hair again, scattering droplets in all directions. I stood, looked around, and just accepted that there was nothing I could do but endure one day at a time. As I walked back to the farm in my damp clothes, Kalinovka was busy evacuating.

Chapter 11: Trenches

While I was away on the abortive effort to defend Crimea, Kalinvoka had been ordered to evacuate—moving all people, animals, and supplies to Grozny. Still dripping, I joined the other new conscripts back at the farm to learn the latest news. Reports of German advances into Russian territory consumed much of the discussion. Everyone was stunned at the speed and extent of destruction. The Russians anticipated that the Germans would be particularly interested in capturing Grozny—and Baku further eastward—because of the vast natural gas and oil reserves.

During that last evening in Kalinvoka, farm managers and soldiers made arrangements to depart for Grozny the following morning. A supply car arrived, and I finally received a standard issue uniform and fresh undergarments. It felt good to wear clean clothes. Holding the heap of dirty clothes, it was hard to believe that I'd worn them for a full year. And yet I could not bear to discard them, however ragged they were; they were my only physical connection to Dubno.

Stepping out of the barn in my fresh attire, I met Jake, who was already bonding with some of the Russian soldiers. I slapped him on the back and cracked a few jokes about how great he looked in uniform. Jake turned with a broad grin, the vodka apparently having an effect on his mood. The bottle passed from one solider to the next, each taking a measured pull. Everyone in Kalinovka was out mingling—saying goodbyes and making plans. There were several groups of soldiers, civilian women gossiping, and a few couples walking, looking for a place to spend the night together.

As we drank and pondered the future, loyal Russian officers gave unabashed expression to their Soviet idealism and taught patriotic songs to the soldiers. The officers' voices rolled in a powerful crescendo as they sang the immensely popular song *Svyashchennaya Voyna* (The Sacred War): "*Vstavay, strana ogromnaya, Vstavay na smertny boy!* (Arise, vast country, Arise for a fight to the death!)" I rolled my eyes at these impromptu indoctrination sessions, but I have to admit that the camaraderie and music would sometimes help groups of despondent soldiers find solace in brotherhood and, occasionally, a feeling of hope. After a few shots of vodka, I, too, was apt to belt out a chorus or two during the war. However, on this last night in Kalinovka, I wandered around looking for anyone who could provide me with news about my friends from Dubno.

Of the group of refugees that had originally arrived at Kalinovka with Jake and me, only the two of us were now together. Groinim had left several days before we returned from the abandoned defense of Crimea. Itzhick and the others had scattered when we fled the train. Groinim and Itzhick were the only two—besides Jake—that I would ever see again (and then not for many years). So, Jake and I made the rounds of Kalinovka, thanking the kind people who had cared for us, privately cursing those that had harassed us—but more than anything seeking news from Poland. The only constant was that the situation was miserable and the outlook bleak. Speculation ran wild about the extent of the German invasion, whether any other nation would intervene to assist, and what Stalin's plans were. Rumor spread of heinous atrocities committed by Germans and Ukrainians.

Early the following morning, Jake and I, carrying guns and meager possessions, joined our unit for the familiar walk to Grozny. As we made our way toward the foothills, I turned back momentarily to look at Kalinovka. The farm seemed smaller than when I'd first arrived. The fields would not be prepared for a harvest this year—and who knew if anyone would ever return to run the farm again? Although glad to be moving on with newfound purpose, I reflected nostalgically: After running breathless for my life, I'd found in Kalinovka a refuge from likely death. It wasn't that life there was easy—work was arduous, food was scarce, and conditions miserable. Still, no bombs exploded, and that in itself was good. I sighed and smiled, turning back toward Grozny.

Walking up the hill, Jake and I recalled our prior trip to Grozny. We laughed about the pail of honey and cursed the girls who stole it. Making our way through the thick and humid forest, we reminisced about our experiences in Kalinovka. Jake asked, "How did it happen again that you were attacked by the bees?"

A month or so after those girls stole the honey from us, I had tried to get some more honey. I hadn't told anyone the story when it happened because the experience had had such a profound effect on me. "Well," I began, "I was out collecting wood for a fire and stopped by the side of the river to wash and have a drink. I took my shirt off and sat on the rocks. A few minutes later, I noticed large birds circling in the sky—vultures." I looked up at Jake.

"So, some animal must have died near the river," Jake said. "What does this have to do with bees?"

"The vultures kept circling," I continued, "and I sat still on the rock looking up at them. After a few moments, they swirled down and perched on the rocks near the riverbed. I looked around to see what they were looking for but couldn't see any dead animal. Then it struck me: They were sitting there looking at me. How terrible must I have looked for them to think I would die? I stood up and tried to shoo one away, but he just stepped away a little, still eyeing me. At this point, I was angry: I roared at them and splashed water toward them, and the birds hopped into the air and flew off. I cursed at them as they flew out of sight, but then sat back down and examined my thin limbs. I knew I was hungry, but I guess I hadn't realized that I looked like I was starving to death.

"It felt like I was staring into a mirror that showed me the horrible truth of how close to death I was. Looking into that reflection, I refused to accept that I was rotting away. At that point, it wasn't that I cared whether I lived or died exactly; I just wasn't going to give up. Those vultures made me defiant. They came to challenge me, to tell me that I couldn't survive. Well, believe you me—I was not going to let them dictate to me."

We continued to walk in silence for a few moments, and then I couldn't help but smile. Jake cracked a small grin. "What's so funny?" he asked.

"So, I was angry," I resumed. "I sat with the pile of firewood at the base of the hills. I kept cursing those vultures. I paced back and forth, convincing myself that I was actually healthy and fit—not gaunt and weak. Turning toward the hillside, I noticed a large beehive hanging from a tree. The thought of the honey jumped out at me immediately. My mouth watered, and I was sure that once the bees scattered, there would be a large pool of honey just waiting for me."

Jake stopped. "No, you didn't..." he said, displaying a toothy grin.

"Yes," I acknowledged between the laughs. "I stood and stared at the hive for several minutes and didn't see any bees flying, so I thought that maybe they were gone. I put down my sticks and selected the longest branch. I wasn't sure exactly where to strike because I didn't want to splatter the honey. So, I decided to hit at the top and knock it off the branch; maybe it wouldn't completely fall apart when it hit the ground. I swung at the top, cleanly knocking the hive down. No sooner had I hit it, *veys mir*, than the bees were everywhere. The hive was broken on the ground, and before I had a chance to reach for the honey, I was stung several times. I ran as fast as I could to the river, and it felt like the bees chased me the entire way. I jumped in and lowered my entire body under the water to hide from the bees and sooth the stings. Once I came out of the water, I sat on a rock and took off my wet clothes to inspect the damage. It hurt like hell but could have been worse."

"Wolf-a-Blinder, only you!" Jake coughed as he laughed. I still smile thinking about how I ran screaming into the river.

We continued chuckling through the forest. There was a mass procession of soldiers and equipment traversing the hills toward Grozny. The hillsides, which had been thick with trees last time we crossed, were now thinned considerably by military units that ravaged the trees for lumber. Every hour or so we would pass another lumber operation—groups of soldiers working tirelessly at cutting down trees and preparing them for transportation. As we passed them, we considered that we might be assigned to the same work. Fatigued and malnourished, the last thing we wanted to do was exhausting manual labor.

Approaching the outskirts of Grozny, our fears were all but confirmed. We noticed mounds of dirt and heard the grunts of back-breaking labor. I hardly recognized the city. The makeshift bazaar had been replaced by military equipment and various defense fortifications. The teenage boys smoking cigarettes and the babushkas with their bundles were gone. Everything was dirty, muddy.

An officer approached us and wearily explained the urgent necessity of establishing defenses against the threat of German tanks. The officer's puffy eyes and stammering speech told us that he hadn't slept in days. Attempting to underscore urgency, he weakly pounded his fist into the palm of his other hand, proclaiming that the Germans must not—will not—acquire Soviet oil and gas. (We didn't know it by name at the time, but the officer was referring to Operation Edelweiss, the German plan authorized by Hitler on July 23, 1942, to capture the oil fields of Baku.) The officer went on to explain that even though we were not on the front lines with Germany, Grozny—and Chechnya generally—was not a safe environment. There was a Chechen insurgency that constantly threatened to undermine the Soviet effort to secure a defensive position—and any soldier who wasn't digging was contending with the rebels.

I was struck by the massive scale of the effort. Dirt moved in all directions. Heaping mounds and vast caverns. It seemed as though every sound was dedicated to digging and building. The officer waved his arm down toward the base of the camp, where he pointed to a stockpile of dirty shovels and ordered us each to take one and start digging trenches. He then divided us into groups and sent us to various points around the outskirts of the city where supervisors would give us more precise instructions.

Clanking and scraping, grunting and shouting. Everyone in Grozny moved with a purpose, and everyone looked miserable. With a collective sigh, we all departed for our respective assignments, spitting curses at the prospect of arduous manual labor. I grabbed my shovel and walked over to a large pile of earth and joined the other men.

An area supervisor barked that he had orders to dig trenches of certain dimensions and that if he failed to reach his targets he would be punished—and as a result, so would we. I stood near the group holding my shovel while the other men drove the spears of their shovels into the ground. The supervisor turned to me. "Who are you, and why the hell are you just standing around?" he demanded.

I snapped to attention. "Vladimir Nusseyonovich, sir, reporting to this unit. We just arrived from Kalinovka."

He ran his thick, dirty hand across his cropped hair. "I don't care who you are. Just dig the damn trenches!" The supervisor stomped off. The soldiers didn't even raise their heads—apparently inured to the supervisor's angry outbursts. I started digging with the others.

Returning to the trenches, the supervisor started to curse as he pointed to a central command car that drove from site to site inspecting progress and issuing orders. As the supervisor cursed to himself, a bookish young officer with an armful of papers called the supervisor over and spread a map across the hood of the car. There were markings and notes scribbled over a geographic map of the area. After they wrapped up their brief conversation, the supervisor returned in an even surlier mood. Apparently, the general responsible for Grozny was not pleased with the progress and had issued stern commands to step up the pace. The supervisor then yelled at all of us to move faster as he stormed away cursing to himself.

It was the middle of the summer. Our workdays were as long as the daylight. The work was monotonous and backbreaking. Provisions were meager. My hands blistered, then calloused. The heat was oppressive. I worked endlessly digging these trenches throughout the summer.

I never became close with the other men working in the trenches. We all hated the job. We would occasionally share dirty jokes to make the time pass more quickly, but the long summer hours took a toll, stripping away any desire for interaction. We mechanically dug each day, complaining with each heap of earth, collapsing each night. Each day I woke hoping that we would be assigned to another job— any job but this one.

Periodically, there would be a need for more lumber to fortify the maze of defenses. I eagerly volunteered to make the day trip into the forest. There were dangers—the insurgency, robbery, or being stranded in the forest with a lame horse—but I was willing to take the risks in exchange for the reprieve from slave labor. My supervisor gave me a list of requirements, which I folded neatly and tucked into my shirt pocket. I then got a horse from the stable and rode for nearly an hour into the forest toward the logging operation.

I never hurried to deliver the lumber orders and I always took longer on the return. Who knew how many more times I would have the opportunity to ride a horse like a free man through the forest? The horse strode through narrow paths hemmed by brush and tall grass as sunlight slanted through the treetops, casting thin, bright rays on the forest floor. I loved those rides. There were stretches where I wouldn't see a single person or hear another voice. Sometimes I would stop the horse just to listen to the forest in silence. Tiny creatures scattering through broken twigs and fallen leaves would rustle the foliage. An odd crack of a branch would echo in the distance. And the faint gurgle of a stream could be heard occasionally if the wind was calm enough not to disturb the leaves.

Alas, my mental escape would never last long. Thudding limbs and a familiar clamor signaled that I was approaching the worksite. Just as in the trenches, these men hunched over equipment, laboring with aching bellies. There was a well-organized system: Trees were cut, stripped, sawed, clipped, and turned into poles and planks. After delivering my lumber orders, I would amble around the piles of limbs and branches to chat with the soldiers. Sharing communal cigarettes, we would swap rumors about war developments and complain about the miserable conditions. Still, we all knew that digging ditches was better than being shot at on the front lines. As the late afternoon heat increased, I'd mount my tired horse and make my way back to Grozny. I would make sure to arrive just before sundown—early enough that my supervisor could account for my presence, but late enough that he wouldn't feel compelled to issue me another order.

Since our sleeping quarters were muggy and hot during the summer, we would usually sleep outside. Jake and I would often meet in the late evening to catch up. He and I had been separated into different units, but we were both equally miserable and hungry. Whenever one of us would manage to find an extra scrap of food, we would share with the other.

We pretty much lived on black bread and *kasha*, boiled buckwheat porridge. Once in a rare while, we would be lucky to find or receive some lard or sausage to add to the *kasha*. *Okroshka* was a staple of the army kitchen—cold soup of raw vegetables, boiled potatoes, meat, and *kvas,* a fermented beverage made from black bread. Vegetables and meat were hard to come by, so *okroshka* was pretty much boiled potato soup and *kvas*. The scarcity of the ingredients due to poor farming practices and German disruption to Soviet supply lines left us with very small rations. To help with the hunger, we drank copious amounts of tea and constantly smoked cigarettes.

Chapter 12:
Patrol

The excruciating labor continued into the fall when the first bite of cold air reminded us of how awful the freezing winter would be. Worn out from months of hard labor, and starving from scarce rations, soldiers occasionally died digging ditches. Our morale, already extremely low, fell ever further with each new report of the intensifying German advance.

In August 1942, German conquest of the Ukraine and the Caucasus seemed inevitable as Germany seemed to take control of additional cities on a daily basis. Worse, the Germans captured Mozdok, just north of Grozny. If other Soviet cities invested as much effort in resistance as we did, and the Germans still cut through effortlessly, how would we be able to stop them? Soviet defensive operations appeared to be completely futile. I could not help but wonder: Was all this effort meaningless? What would happen to me if I was captured by the Germans?

As the Germans advanced ever closer, we continued to dig and build endlessly. No matter how extensive the network of channels, or how high the mounds, there always seemed to be more dirt to move, more walls to retain. My hands were calloused and cracked. My over-strained and undernourished joints and muscles ached. I saw several soldiers collapse from exhaustion and dehydration; some never recovered and died in the infirmary.

The Terek River afforded the Soviets an opportunity to slow the advancing Germans, who were stretched too far forward for their reinforcements and supplies to support them. The foxholes and trenches were finally completed, which meant reassignment of personnel. Supply lines needed additional support. Munitions depots and base facilities needed to be monitored at all times. Jake and I each received orders to join a team of soldiers guarding the base in scheduled rotations throughout the week. The work was monotonous and boring but a welcome change from hard labor.

The German advance slowed, but they were still at our doorstep. Not more than a month into my new assignment, the Germans were stopped short of Vladikavkaz. The Germans then bombed the Grozny oil fields, sending black plumes of smoke towering into the sky. Fortunately, the turn of seasons further slowed the Germans. It was clear they weren't planning—or weren't able—to advance further through the cold. Winter was a mixed blessing: Instead of fighting the German soldiers, we would fight to stay warm—but at least the Germans would come no closer, and occasionally the Soviets would be able to successfully target and destroy pockets of German soldiers along their critical supply lines.

Those late fall and early winter months were full of uncertainty. Near Grozny, the war reached a strange stalemate. The Battle for Stalingrad raged on, but here at the edge of the German advance, the war pulled back like backwater from a wave. Still, we were on high alert against German plots or Chechen insurgents, so we worked around the clock on constant patrols.

I came to enjoy the morning shifts. The cold pinched my cheeks but would dissipate with the first light. The sun would rise to reveal a tapestry of gold, auburn, and red leaves blanketing the mud-covered ground. Night shifts were equally serene in their own way, affording hours of time to stargaze. In fact, we spent so much time studying the night sky that we reached a point where we could determine how far along into our shifts we were based on the position of the stars. In addition to these natural distractions, the routine patrols allowed plenty of time to chat with the people of the town.

I befriended a few of the young teenage boys, who became quite clever at finding goods to trade. They would steal from one group of soldiers and then trade with another. During one of my patrols, I caught one of them pilfering a supply bin that wasn't properly secured. The boy pleaded with me not to turn him in or punish him. I told him that I wouldn't punish him as long as he told me what he planned to do with the supplies. He then introduced me to a small group of other boys. Once the others saw me with him, they panicked. I started to laugh, calming them down some. We made a deal: They would provide me with extra cigarettes and I wouldn't get them in trouble. This arrangement worked out pretty well—I had more to smoke or trade, and they avoided a beating.

Then there were the girls. I felt sorry for many of them. They were desperate, hungry, cold, and had families that suffered. Many of the young ladies would try to befriend Soviet soldiers in order to receive some extra supplies. Plenty of the soldiers took advantage of the opportunity to enjoy some companionship with these young ladies. I guess the soldiers and ladies each got what they wanted. Personally, I made friends with a few girls that were able to trade goods. Cigarettes from the boys were great, but if I wanted a pair of socks or spread of jam, the boys were useless. The girls, however, were great at finding these. So, I traded the cigarettes from the boys for supplies from the girls.

As welcome as these trades were, they were relatively infrequent. Most days were filled with long hours of stress, uncertainty, and, above all, hunger. One cold night in early winter, I was assigned to work a night shift. Sleep was our only temporary escape from constant hunger and being awake at night with no diversions to keep my mind off of food only made things worse. I took short naps where I could, but the only way to stay warm was to keep moving, so I could not fully rest, stay warm, or—as my stomach rumbled constantly—forget about food for long. I can understand why some people just died; they couldn't handle this constant struggle and quit.

Judging by the position of the stars, I was halfway through my shift when the scent of bread baking struck my senses. At first, I thought I was delusional. No one was awake, and the base and town were quiet. Consumed with the smell, I sniffed deeply to take it all in, imagining the taste of a fresh loaf. I quickly pushed the thought out of my head, refusing to torture myself any further. I rubbed my hands together to stay warm and continued on my patrol.

I walked only a few paces before being struck again by the potent smell of bread. This time, my mouth watered, and I was certain that my senses weren't deceiving me. Turning a corner on my patrol, I noticed a dim light emanating from a shop that once functioned as a bakery. I proceeded closer to the shop, now fully convinced that the smell came from within.

It would be unusual for a civilian to be out in the middle of the night, so I was apprehensive about who I might find inside the building. I held my gun with both hands and observed from a close distance. As I considered whether to approach the shop or inform an officer, the light suddenly went out and a man crept out of the front door, stuffing a package inside his coat.

The smell of the bread was all-consuming at this point. I trained my gun on the man and ordered, "*Stoi ne smecte!* (Don't move!)" The man froze, raising his hands in the air, causing the package to fall to the ground. He and I both stared down at the package—steam wafting into the cold air—uncertain what to do next. Noticing my gun, the man implored me not to shoot. He admitted sneaking into the old bakery to make bread, knowing that it was not his shop. He then offered it to me, begging not to be reported. I couldn't have cared less about rules and regulations; I just wanted the bread.

"*Davai suda* (Give it here)," I told the man. He tossed the package to me. I picked up the package with one hand, keeping the other on the gun, pointed at the man. He stood there, shivering, with his hands up. I looked at the package and then the man. I wanted to laugh, but forced myself to keep a straight face. "*Von atzudah!* (Scram!)" I barked, flicking my gun at the man for him to leave. I didn't have to tell him twice. "Thank you, thank you," the man mumbled as he stumbled over his feet and ran off.

Standing there with the warm bread in my hands, I looked up at the stars and realized I had another problem. My shift was nearing the end, and if I was caught with the bread, I would be punished; they would think I had abandoned my responsibilities and snuck into the bakery to make the bread while on patrol. I took the bread from the package and held it close. The hard crust and spongy texture felt wonderful in my hands. In reality, it was an awful hodgepodge of straw and flour, confected from whatever ingredients the man in the old bakery had managed to find. Still, I could only imagine a delicious woven challah from my childhood.

Not wasting another moment, I walked away from the buildings to stand in the shadows out of sight of anyone who might walk by. I slung the gun back over my shoulder and tore the clumpy loaf in half. Holding the crust with both hands, I raised the loaf to my mouth and felt the warmth near my face. Smiling, I sank my teeth into the center of the loaf, taking a large bite out of the bread. It was bland and gritty but warm and satiating. My stomach rumbled as I quickly devoured the bread. Chewing on the last remaining grains, I wrapped the second half of the bread and tucked it away in my pocket.

The following evening, Jake and I managed to find a little time to catch up. We met near our sleeping quarters and walked aimlessly around the base. "Yasha," I said. "Do I have a surprise for you!"

Curious, Jake raised a thick eyebrow. I proceeded to tell him about my experience the prior night, and carefully passed him the piece of bread wrapped in the cloth. "*Dikar!* (Wild man!)" he said with a wry smile. "Only you would have the nerve to take the bread!" Laughing, he slapped a pack of cigarettes into my palm. "Just don't ask how I got that," he chuckled. We strolled and laughed about the bread story while Jake gnawed on the hard roll.

Swallowing the last bite of the stolen bread, Jake asked, "Any news from Dubno?" Inhaling my cigarette, I shook my head. "I didn't expect so." Jake slumped.

"I overheard the commanders discussing the German advance," Jake said, changing the subject. "One senior officer complained that morale was very low; few had hope of survival, even fewer of victory." I wasn't surprised to hear this assessment. Depression was fairly common among the line soldiers.

"So, what should we do, if the Germans reach Grozny?" I asked.

Jake paused to think, taking a long drag of my cigarette. "As I see it, the Russians and Germans will see us only as Jews. They won't care about our uniform. So, we are better off running as refugees than staying to fight as Russian soldiers."

We crouched down to draw a crude map on the ground. "We are stuck between the Black Sea and Caspian Sea," I said. "We can't go north or west."

Jake considered the situation. "Baku" he suggested. "We could go to Baku in order to find a way into Iran. From Iran, hopefully seek asylum in British-occupied Palestine."

We stared at our scratches in the earth, looked at each other, and shrugged. It couldn't be worse than our current situation. We agreed:

If the Germans were on the verge of taking Grozny, we'd make our way to Baku. Standing up, I smeared away the map with my shoe. The sun was setting, and Jake and I needed to get back for the night shift. He thanked me for the bread, and I him for the smokes. We were lucky to have one another.

I spent the remaining months of 1942 conducting monotonous patrols, seeking contraband food, and chatting with Jake whenever possible. As it turned out, there was a battle in the north that was profoundly instrumental in determining whether I would flee as a refugee or remain in the fight: the Battle of Stalingrad August, 1942, through February, 1943. The success of the Russian Army during this battle separated the German fronts from their supply lines, galvanizing the morale of Russian soldiers, who now believed that defeating the Germans was possible. The reality began to set in that Grozny would be safe from German attack—the countless trenches would thankfully remain as barren gashes in the city outskirts and not gravesites for fallen soldiers.

In early 1943, all of the soldiers in the Grozny area gathered for an announcement. The Red Army was making stunning progress in recapturing German-held cities. Given the changing tide in the war, the Russian Army made preparations to take the fight to the Germans. Defensive patrols would come to an end, and just in time, too—the vicious Russian winter was already causing numerous deaths due to exposure. Resources from Grozny would be reallocated to recapture lost cities and push the Germans out of the Soviet Union. This news was met with broad support by the soldiers, most of whom—exhausted from digging and freezing—were eager to fight back. Following the meeting, we reported to our commanding officers for our new orders.

Chapter 13:
Communications Officer

I had to report to my new command by the end of the day. I collected my belongings and eventually found Jake packing up to leave for his new assignment. He seemed anxious.

"I am going to the front," Jake said, staring down at his belongings. The words hung in the air; the gravity of those words weighed heavily on us. We'd been in constant danger since fleeing Dubno, but somehow we'd carried on with a sense of invincibility. At the same time, we both realized that, until now, we hadn't been forced to hold a position against a German attack and remain fighting to the death. "*Ni shagu nazad* (Not one step back)," Jake said absently, referencing Stalin's Order No. 227 prohibiting soldiers from retreating from a position.

Although neither of us said so, we both knew that the chances of surviving at the front were low. We contemplated the awful possibility that we might never see one another again, causing a long awkward silence. The fact that I didn't immediately respond with the same assignment made it evident to Jake that he and I were about to part ways. I was worried that he might resent me for not going to fight along with him. I felt guilty that he would be forced to face the worst alone.

Jake rose, striking a match and lighting cigarettes for us both. "I am assigned to infantry. At least I'll have a chance to kill those German bastards," Jake said, smiling dimly. Pointing to the paper in my hand, he asked, "*Nu*, what paradise did you get?"

I unfolded the order and read, "Communications."

"*Wolf-a-Blinder!* Communications...! G-d help us all!" Jake howled with laughter. "Just don't send my location to the Germans!"

Jake continued laughing and teasing me, and I couldn't resist; I laughed along with him. Jake was a *mensch*. He could have resented me. He could have been envious and angry and cruel. But he wasn't. He was graceful. He was actually happy for me. It made me feel even more guilty.

The humor relieved the tension. Jake was right. It was ironic. Here I was—the most likely to be clumsy or to overlook the obvious—with responsibilities in communications.

"If I'm in communications, maybe I'll be able to check on your location?" I ventured. Jake nodded and sighed. We stood there for a moment smoking quietly, the smoke wafting in the air between us. I didn't dare say a word until Jake was ready to speak. Jake took one more deep drag, slowly exhaling the smoke. He flicked the smoldering butt into the mud, signaling his readiness to depart. Jake looked me square in the eyes, placed both hands on my shoulders, and said, "*Zei gezunt.*"

I could hardly stand to return his look, but I did. I had to. Holding back tears, we embraced. "*Zei gezunt,*" I responded. Jake collected his belongings and we walked out together. It would be two years before I would receive a reliable update about Jake, but I'll come back to that later.

People were crisscrossing the base in all directions, each making their way toward the next phase of this war. I stood there in the middle of the base, reading my orders: Communications Officer, Mines and Ordinances. I didn't feel the same urgency that seemed to drive the others around me, but with nothing else to do, I walked to my new command.

Reporting to the central command office, I showed my papers to a clerk, who pointed me in the direction of the colonel in charge of my unit—Colonel Konenov. The Colonel was a middle-aged man with a casual and calm air. A stack of papers was neatly arranged on one side of his desk; ornaments and personal memorabilia decorated the other half. Next to his desk was a small table, topped with a half-empty bottle of vodka and a few dirty glasses. He was signing some papers for a clerk when I entered. Completing the final signature, he waved me in.

I presented myself, announcing my name, saluting, and reporting for duty. The Colonel saluted back and reviewed my papers. He gave me a long look and nodded in what I hoped was approval. I was suddenly nervous, as one wrong answer could have me transferred to the front.

"Vladimir Nusseyonovich," he pronounced slowly. He must have noticed my muddled accent and choppy Russian. After Polish and Yiddish, Russian was my third language. "Where are you from?" he asked without looking up from his paper. I explained the story of how I'd fled Poland and joined the army in Kalinovka.

The Colonel peered over his papers, gave me another long look, and smiled. "*Maladetz* (Good job), we need more soldiers with determination to survive," he said. He invited me to sit as he eased into his chair across from me and began to explain my responsibilities.

"I report to Lieutenant General Konstantin Koroteev and am responsible for four platoons tasked with planting and removing land mines," he explained. "As my communications officer, I will need you to manage my communications regarding mine activity between HQ and field bases. There are several communications officers working for this unit, and our focus will be to clear mines as quickly as possible to advance against the Germans." The Colonel paused and studied me further. "*Ni shagu nazad!* (Not one step back!)" he quoted Stalin's Order No. 227. "*Panyatana?* (Understood?)"

I nodded, well aware of the *shtrafbats*—penal battalions used to punish criminals or retreating soldiers. Worse yet was "trampler" duty. Tramplers were forced to run side by side across known German minefields in advance of an assault. *Shtrafniks* that resisted or avoided their orders were either summarily executed or assigned to trampler duty. Due to how awful the deaths were, being a trampler was actually worse than being quickly executed. Tramplers injured by a mine blast were left to die on the battlefield as Red Army soldiers continued forward, stepping over the fallen tramplers. The Soviets had inferior war materiel and weak logistical organization, but they had a deep supply of soldiers and nationalistic will. The Soviet strategy was darkly called *pishichnaya myaca* (meat grinder): Millions of Russian men, ill-equipped to be soldiers, served adequately as a human barrier, absorbing German bullets to slow the German advance and pave the way for Soviet counterattack.

"HQ has already deployed *shtrafbats* to our location," the Colonel said, "which we will use as part of our tactical approach to support operations. There will be *shtrafniks* that will try to avoid their duty. We will use them as tramplers to clear mines." The Colonel paused, turned toward the bottle of vodka and poured a shot in each glass, leaving the two glasses on the table. "Understand this, Vladimir Nusseyonovich," he resumed, "I manage critical and sensitive operations. Implementing orders to clear mines is not pleasant, but it must be done to protect our fighting soldiers and give the Soviet Union the best chance at victory. I need to know that I can trust you will fulfill your orders. Know this: If you fail to follow orders, you might find *yourself* assigned to a *shtrafbat*."

The threat of being shipped to a *shtrafbat* was about as bad as it could get. I hoped he didn't notice the sweat beading on my forehead as I tried to remain calm. I remember clearing my throat, trying to hide my nerves. I mustered up as much confidence as I could. "Sir, I am committed to the fight against the Germans and will faithfully fulfill my orders," I said.

The Colonel gave me another long look and reached for the glasses on his side table. He handed me one of the glasses, rose to toast, and shouted, "*Pobeda!*" Standing up with a nervous laugh, I echoed the toast, and flicked the glass back to swallow the vodka in a single shot.

The Colonel invited me to stay a little while longer as we chatted about personal backgrounds and interests. I don't remember exactly what we discussed; I was just relieved that he didn't change my orders and send me to the front, or worse. The topic of my religion didn't come up, but I suspect that he knew right away that I was Jewish. He wanted to make sure that I would be loyal and follow his orders, which I promised to do. He went on to detail his expectations of me, making sure I was literate and capable of managing the responsibilities.

Following this short conversation, the Colonel pulled out a sheet of paper and drafted an order for me to acquire a new ID card. Leaning back in his chair, he explained that I would need an ID that authorized blanket approval for transportation and use of communications systems so that I could efficiently conduct the Colonel's business. I nodded, not realizing what a gift this ID would prove to be.

It turned out that Jake's platoon was assigned to work closely with mine operations, which allowed me to always know Jake's location. Unfortunately, it would not be possible to know whether he was safe or hurt, as I knew only the location of the platoon's movements and not the status of individual soldiers.

The job required constant travel between command posts, relaying messages and maps. Each trip was fraught with risk: German attack, criminals, mines, and worst of all—potential capture with sensitive information. My ID authorized me to acquire any provisions I needed to complete my mission and to use any method of transportation available. Since I reported directly to the Colonel, I also had some relative autonomy that other soldiers with multi-tiered command structures did not.

I worked tirelessly throughout the first part of 1943. The winter was brutally cold and food was scarce. It was a constant battle against hunger, against exposure, and against the Germans. During those first months, however, my greatest fear was upsetting the Colonel. I knew that if I developed a good relationship with him and earned his trust, I would give myself at least a chance to make it through the war. The Colonel had no tolerance for excuses; if he issued an order, he expected that order to be fully executed. I had seen him reassign other staff for failing to meet his expectations; all of them ended up in dangerous frontline positions. I'll never forget the first time I saw it happen.

Nearly a week into my new assignment, a soldier appeared before the Colonel to report the outcome of a mission—holding the same pouch the Colonel had asked him to deliver. The soldier explained that he hadn't known exactly where to go with the message and was scared of being captured by the Germans. The Colonel paused to examine the soldier, who stood unapologetically before him. The Colonel asked if the soldier had asked field commanders for directions, or if he'd familiarized himself with maps, or if he'd done anything to help himself succeed. The soldier answered each question with a sheepish "No." The Colonel grunted, pulled out a sheet of paper, and scribbled some orders. He stood, calmly, and handed the orders to the soldier. He looked him squarely in the eyes. "I see that communications are too difficult for you," he said, without raising his voice. "Not to worry—here is an order that you will easily be able to follow." The Colonel called his sergeant over, then turned to the soldier. "Collect all your belongings, and report to the field post," he ordered. "Their unit deploys to the front this afternoon. Your job will be clear: Shoot at the Germans." Before the soldier could protest, the sergeant escorted him away. I learned the lesson well: Do my job.

I made sure that no matter the circumstances, I accomplished my missions—large or small. I studied the maps. I developed relationships with the field commanders and munitions supervisors. I learned how to drive trucks and how to ride horses. I improved my Russian, learning the key vocabulary I needed to do the Colonel's business. With each successful mission, I gradually earned the Colonel's confidence.

Sensing the Colonel's growing trust, I focused less on how long it took me to complete a mission and more on ensuring that it was done. If a mission should take a day to complete, I would take two. I developed relationships with civilians with access to black market goods, just as I had with the teenage boys and girls in Grozny. Occasionally, I would secretly bring in some extra items to share with the Colonel—cigarettes, jam, or a piece of smoked meat.

The Colonel appreciated my dedication—and the extras I would acquire during my missions. Whenever I brought a delicacy back, he would promptly pour me a drink and invite me to share in the treat. We developed a friendly relationship over these drinking sessions. The Colonel opened up a bit personally, talking about his family and background. He came from a prominent military family but took more pleasure in personal interests such as art, culture, and chess. Most of all, the Colonel adored the company of women. He talked often about his conquests, pursuit of Muscovite women, and plans to marry into an established family.

While serving in field command, the Colonel somehow managed to always find a girlfriend in each town. After learning about his girlfriends, I would make sure to trade for a gift that he could give them: a blouse, a scarf, even some perfume. The Colonel loved it. Each time I brought him something for a girlfriend, his face would light up. Doing my job well and offering the Colonel some contraband items bought me goodwill. The Colonel didn't micromanage my work; he cared only about results. This left me with some limited freedom and extra time I used to visit with soldiers and civilians to learn about their experiences.

I could relate intimately to the stories so many of these people told. Like me, they'd narrowly escaped the German assault, often fleeing with just the clothes on their backs. The soldiers all said how overwhelmed and outmatched they were initially—and all privately admitted they were grateful to have fled before Stalin's Order 227 because authorized retreats were now few and far between. Occasionally, I would hear a story of someone that had been stranded under German control and managed to escape.

The violence and chaos unleashed by a German assault deeply scarred those who survived—forced to leave loved ones, to watch family, friends, and comrades killed by bullets, mortars, crumbling debris. Those who witnessed the atrocities of the Germans (and their local collaborators) after the initial assault were profoundly affected by the unimaginable evil. It was difficult to comprehend the stories I heard: the scale of the devastation, the extent of the cruelty. I would often hear about the political side of the war—the frustration with the Soviets, Ukrainian pursuit of national independence through collaboration with Germany. More quietly, there was fear of Stalin and the NKVD, the Soviet internal secret police. I would hear about a brother or son summarily shot for disobeying Stalin's commands. The worst stories were the ones about civilian murders. Time and time again, I would hear about mass graves and massacres.

One of the worst atrocities I heard about occurred outside Kiev, in a ravine called Babi Yar. The story went that approximately 100,000 people were killed by the SS and the Ukrainian Police. Civilians were rounded up like cattle, forced out of Kiev, then murdered in mass graves.[xii] I had witnessed death: by starvation, exposure, gunfire and mortars. But the organized murder of 100,000 people? Mass graves of civilians? It was difficult to imagine the sheer scale and magnitude of such horror. I didn't doubt that civilian casualties occurred. However, given that these stories were all passed through word of mouth, I was certain that there must have been some exaggeration. Terrible tragedies certainly, but mass murders in the tens—no, hundreds—of thousands? I found the reports hard to believe. Years later, I would learn that not only was it all true—it was much, much worse.

While my job had its advantages, war was unimaginably horrific. Mine detection became a massive effort. As the Germans retreated from Soviet cities, they left mines behind to slow the Soviet offensive. Soviet mines littered the roads in an effort to hinder the German assault. Occasionally, we would be tasked with a tactical deployment of mines as part of an attack on a German position. However, since the end of the Battle of Stalingrad, the overall focus was on detecting and defusing the thousands of mines scattered across the Soviet Union.

Our platoons used metal detectors or, for the Germans' wooden mines, dogs to identify the mines. The detection and defusing process was subject to the pace of attack the Soviet commanders required. If we could afford a longer period of time for some strategic process, we would try to clear the mines methodically. However, at this point in the war, we sensed an opportunity to push the Germans back. So, the commanders deployed *shtrafbats* to march ahead of our infantry.

When our infantry was planning an advance, I would relay the Colonel's orders to both the infantry and penal battalion commanders to mobilize *shtrafniks*. These penal battalions, often unarmed, were forced to march ahead by armed guards behind them and shot if they refused to charge into certain danger. They were all dead men walking. The look in their eyes, much like their predicament, was hopeless. Since refusing to obey orders as a *shtrafnik* would result in summary execution, most of the *shtrafniks* charged ahead as ordered, since their best chance (however remote) for survival lay in avoiding death on the battlefield. For every few *shtrafniks* that survived, hundreds of thousands of others were brutally maimed, left to die agonizing deaths in the mud. I witnessed countless deaths. I witnessed thousands of Soviet troops step over the writhing bodies and pools of streaming blood as we fought on, searching for a way to turn the tide of the war.

Chapter 14:
A Letter from Dubno

By the summer of 1943, the German army was stretched thin, and the Soviet advance was gaining momentum. We were well on the way to retaking most of central Ukraine. There was a hint of optimism among the Russian troops that the Germans could be defeated.

We remained in Krasnodar through the latter half of the summer, running operations from our base there. Krasnodar was in ruins. Bodies of murdered civilians, soldiers, and partisans lay burned in the streets or left hanging in trees. That summer, the Soviets began trials, including of their own citizens, for collusion with the Nazis and for participation in war crimes. Trials of collaborators accused of assisting the Germans resulted in either capital punishment of imprisonment.[xiii]

Wandering around Krasnodar, I saw Jewish cemeteries desecrated, corpses of Jews with bloodied Stars of David wrapped around their arms, and piles of murdered Jews—apparently all shot together. I ached when I saw these scenes and immediately thought of the stories I'd heard about civilian massacres. It was an awful paradox: There was hope at last that we might turn the tide of the war, but I was increasingly hopeless that I would have anything to return to if we prevailed. The bodies in the streets, the mass graves; this wasn't just a war of territorial conquest. The Germans were targeting the Jews deliberately, killing them just because they were Jews. I burned with hatred against the Germans and their collaborators. I could not help but fear that Dubno would look similar to Krasnodar. As painful as it was to think of Dubno in ruins, I realized that with the Soviet advance I might be able to return to Dubno one day. So, I decided to write a letter.

The thought of writing had never really entered my mind until then. I was always on missions, or running, or trying to stay warm, or trying to eat. There was always something. I knew it was possible to write, but to whom? I kept putting it off. I guess I was afraid that I wouldn't receive a response— and also afraid of what I might find out if I did.

It was during a driving afternoon rain when I finally sat down to write. I found a corner in an old government building. A segment of the entranceway was reduced to rubble, but the building was in generally sound condition. Water flowed outside the front of the building, pooling near the entrance and spilling into the stone-floored foyer. The rhythm of the raindrops on the roof beat louder and faster, diverting my attention. I was distracted easily since I wasn't sure where to begin the letter or what to say. Home was always in the back of my mind but somewhere off in the distance. Even when I discussed Dubno with Jake, it was something unattainable—a life that was no longer mine. I was now confronted with reconciling the life I'd once had with my life in the army—and I struggled to envision what possible future there could be.

Refocusing, I stared at the blank page and noticed a wet spot where a drop had landed on the page. Wiping the water with the palm of my hand, I took a deep breath and decided that the simpler the letter, the better. I addressed the letter to the Dubno *gorsovet,* or city hall. I stated my name, listed the names of my family members, and included instructions on where to send a response. Thinking of Jake, I mentioned that he too was alive—as far as I knew. I sat there staring at the page, wondering if I should include any more information about myself or ask any more questions about my family. I tapped the page a few times with my pen, leaving a few dots on the margins as I let my mind wander in thought. Another few drops fell on my hand, splashing lightly on the page, prompting me to shake the page dry. I would leave the letter just as it was. I folded the page, slid it into the envelope, and tucked it in my pocket. Protecting the letter, I darted out of the building through puddled, muddy streets to send it as quickly as possible.

Standing at the postal center, I looked at the sealed envelope in my hand and weighed whether to send it. Of course I wanted to know the fate of my family, and I hoped for the best—but I feared the worst. I knew that it would take a long time for the letter to reach anyone and much longer to receive a response. I might not receive a response at all. I sighed, dropped the letter in the outgoing mail, and walked back into the rain.

I needed something to take my mind off Dubno. I knew just where to go — the Colonel. After the Krasnodar trials, the local population did whatever they could to curry favor with the military commanders. This made trading for goods easier, and I stocked up on supplies, including a few special items for the Colonel. I never knew when I would have an opportunity to collect trinkets for his mistresses, so I always made sure I had something set aside in case I needed to stay in his good graces. I had several French silk neck scarfs, all adorned with contemporary designs and oh-so-chic. I carefully removed one from its hidden location in my field bag and went to see the Colonel.

The Colonel was alone, poring over maps and paperwork. Entering with a mischievous smile, I saluted, waiting for him to invite me over. He glanced up, waved me over, and returned to reviewing his papers. "What can I do for you, Vladimir?" he asked without looking up. I presented the scarf to him and said with a smile, "For Miss Krasnodar." He looked at the scarf, put away his pen, and laughed. He ran his fingers over the fine fabric and leaned back in his chair, smiling broadly. "This is perfect, Vladimir! Thank you very much!" The Colonel was like a boy. I could practically read his thoughts—his pleasure in visualizing giving the gift to his lady and the reward that would come after. He tucked away the scarf and chuckled. I stood, ready to leave, when—on cue—he asked, "Would you like a drink?"

"Only if you are planning on having one," I responded courteously but expectantly. The Colonel loved talking about ladies. And this time I pretended to be especially interested. I even chimed in about how wonderful it would be to see a beautiful woman wearing nothing but the scarf and a fur coat. Oh, he roared with delight! We toasted to each of his conquests. He loved reliving each one, and before long, we were both thoroughly drunk. The Colonel broke out a few treasured delicacies, and as we shared the savory slices of smoked meat and salted herring, I somehow managed—between the stories, the food, and the vodka—to forget my sorrow. Mission accomplished.

Nearly two months passed with no response from Dubno; I trudged on all the while with the rest of the Soviet advance, dragging the weight of uncertainty along with me. We left Krasnodar, pressing north toward Rostov-na-Donu and Dnipropetrovsk. The plan was to make our way to Kharkiv, Poltava—all cities that I'd fled several years before. The rubble and remnants of the destroyed towns gave mute testimony to the atrocities they'd witnessed. Lost and frail souls wandered the streets or huddled in hovels.

Each time I was instructed to carry an order, I made time to speak with some of the survivors. They all told horrible tales of murder and destruction. I was reluctant to ask specifically about Jews, uncertain about the consequences of the query. But it was ominous that I did not see one civilian Jew. Worse, the symbols of Jewish life in each city were destroyed: synagogues, shops, and cemeteries. Despite this, it was hard to tell the difference between general destruction of Soviet towns and the targeted destruction of Jewish property. It would be another six months before I would encounter a civilian Jewish survivor and learn first-hand what happened.

I still had no word from Dubno. I knew to expect some delay from the *polvaya pochta*, a central mail system that routed all mail to and from soldiers through an anonymous military address so as to conceal the location of our bases. But it seemed hopeless; I doubted I would ever hear back. I tried to put the thought of a response out of my head, resolving that at some point in the future, if I were to survive this war, I would return to Dubno and search for my family. Then, it arrived.

I had just returned from a mission outside Dnipropetrovsk and was tired from the long, sleepless days. I was informed that we would be moving further west toward Bessarabia in the morning. Just as I was about to lie down to recover, I noticed an envelope on my mat. I figured it was a request from the Colonel, so I casually reached to pick it up with a chuckle, thinking he needed a gift for another girl. I flipped the envelope over and was jolted to attention: The letter was from Dubno.

I was sitting alone under a makeshift tarp tent, trembling with the envelope in my hand. I'm not sure why, but I looked around to make sure I was alone—free from any source of interruption. I eased myself down to the floor and shifted closer to the candlelight. Thoughts raced through my mind. If I'd received a response, that must mean that there was good news, right? Why else would I receive a letter? If everyone had been killed, surely no one would write back. Optimism grew within me. This was going to be good news.

I nervously opened the letter, finding it difficult to focus on the words I was reading. The letter was from one of my cousins, Jake's brother, Aaron Grossberg. I thought, "If he is alive, then my family must be too!" Aaron wrote that Stanislaw, the same Polish official who knew my family, had staffed the city hall during the German occupation. Stanislaw had received my letter and, recognizing my name, had passed it along to Aaron and then sent Aaron's response to me.

Aaron's explanation about how he received the letter seemed irrelevant, almost as though he was stalling, but I needed to read every word. He wrote that he was grateful that both Jake and I were alive. The letter rambled on about how he hoped we were doing well and staying safe. I was losing my patience—where was the news about my family? At last, Aaron got around to the Jews of Dubno. His account was very general, but he mentioned that the Ukrainians and Nazis had murdered nearly all of the Dubno Jews. And then I read these words: "Wolf, I am so sorry to inform you, but your entire family was killed." I dropped the paper.

Everything inside of me burned and ached. All I could think about was my brother, begging to ride on the bicycle with me—and how I so dismissively turned him down. *Nemah an rameh...*I tore at my hair and clothes. Why, why didn't I just let him join me? If he'd come with me, he would be alive now! I thought of my mother, standing in the doorway. I shook with anger, with grief. My father, my mother, my sister, my brother. All gone. I left home and am now alone. At that moment, I hated everyone and everything. Filled with rage, I clenched my fists and cursed. I curled over to my knees and pounded the dirt until I had no more strength and the tears blurred my vision. I sobbed, crouched, and fell on my mat. Eventually, my battered hands wiped away the tears, and I picked up the paper again to read the remainder of the letter through puffy eyes. The letter concluded with words of condolence and a sad statement that the Dubno I left was gone. Aaron wished me well and asked me to send regards to Jake.

I sat numb for the rest of evening, contemplating my life. Since fleeing my home, I'd never had the time to actually care whether I lived or died; I blindly ran and fought and struggled. The thought of reuniting with my family always filled me with some hope, even though I understood that such hope could be in vain. Now, I just felt empty. The only thought that drove me was to beat the Germans down as violently as possible. I hated them. I hated the Ukrainians. I hated this war. How could there be a G-d that would allow such misery?

Chapter 15:
Missions

The next couple months were a blur. I mindlessly drifted through my routines, and can hardly recall what I did or where I was. Gradually, a nagging thought entered my mind: What if Aaron was wrong? How did he know that all of my family members were dead? Did he witness their murders? I knew my sister was already outside of Dubno when I left—how did Aaron know about her? I convinced myself that Aaron probably assumed they were all dead since most of Dubno's Jews had been murdered. But, if *he* was alive, perhaps my family was too—maybe hiding in the forest, in someone's home, or maybe they'd managed to run away, just as I had. I resolved that I would go to Dubno as soon as possible to search for my family myself and learn firsthand what had happened.

By mid-1943, there was more frequent discussion in army ranks about the Allies opening a second front. Germany feared a strong Western Front because the battle with the Russians in the east left them stretched thin and vulnerable. Eventually, the Western Front did open, nearly a year later. Everyone agreed that the second front weakened and contributed to the ultimate defeat of the Germans. But it was also widely believed that the action was taken far too late. It was well known among the Russian soldiers that Winston Churchill loathed communism, and many of them suspected the Allies had deliberately waited until the Russians were exhausted from war before opening the second front.

Among the Jews serving in the Soviet Army, we had our own reasons for resenting the Allied delay. We felt that if the Western Front had been opened sooner, millions of Jews and others would have been spared senseless death. After the war, we were incensed to learn that the Allies could have bombed the rail lines to prevent further mass murders of Jews in extermination camps but refused to do so.

Waiting for a second front to open in order to ease the struggle on the Eastern Front was a luxury the Soviets could not afford. Weary Russian soldiers plodded onward, heading west across farm and village and town to liberate occupied lands. Some cities offered minimal resistance and were easily liberated; others could take weeks to overcome. German prisoners of war were captured, others killed—all with businesslike efficiency. A base camp was established in each city to proclaim liberation—at least symbolically. We pushed on like this for several months, liberating cities, fighting pockets of resistance, often mounted by local collaborators no less ruthless than the Germans they served. It all boiled down to numbers: The Soviets kept throwing young men against these enemies, ultimately wearing them down.

The further we pressed, the more desperate the Germans became—and the more dangerous my missions. The Germans planted mines and deployed snipers to hinder communications channels, disrupting message relays. Several of my colleagues were killed trying to relay messages between command posts. I barely escaped with my life on more than one occasion when sniper fire nearly stopped me for good. By this point in the war, I had conducted more missions than I could recall—all risky but usually routine. I knew where I was going and what to do. But there was one mission that stood out from the rest.

It was early fall, 1943. We hit significant pockets of resistance near Bessarabia. Germans and their local collaborators were deeply entrenched throughout the region, leaving only narrow passages from one Soviet base to another. The Colonel called me late in the day and briefed me on a mission I would need to embark on later that night.

Handing me a sealed pouch, the Colonel said, "Vladimir, there is a small secret base camp at the front line. I am not permitted to inform you where this base is or how to get there." Pointing to another officer in the room, he explained, "Uri will take you to a horse that knows the way there. You will ride the horse until you arrive at the base, deliver the package to the commanding officer, and return here. You must set off promptly upon nightfall because there is a chance you could be spotted during daylight."

I held the package in my hands and looked at the Colonel and Uri. Sensing my uncertainty, the Colonel laughed and waved me off. "Everything will be fine, don't worry," he said. "Go with Uri before it gets too late." I wouldn't have worried, except that was the first time he ever told me not to worry.

Uri escorted me to a stable, where he brought out a saddled horse. I asked if the horse really knew where it was going. And if the horse fell or became injured or if there was an attack, where should I go? Uri said I had nothing to worry about: The horse knew the directions. He said that to protect the location of the secret base in the event of German capture, very few people knew the location. Unconvinced, but with no alternative, I nodded and mounted the horse. Uri whispered to the horse, handed me the reins and left.

Under cover of darkness, I set off on my mission. I had conducted numerous missions: in daylight, at night, in groups, alone—but I had always known where I was going. It was an eerie feeling sitting passively as a passenger on a horse and trusting it to take the correct path. The only control I had was to slow the horse or speed it up. The horse walked toward a path that led into the woods, leaving the base camp to disappear behind me. I started to feel nervous, the sound of my heartbeat drowning out the clopping hooves.

I was told that the entire trip would take a couple hours—which alone on a horse near enemy lines felt much, much longer. The horse eased his way along a trail, circumventing fallen logs and thickets, as though he had walked this path a thousand times before. Skirting the edge of a ravine, I heard voices. Tightening the reins, I stopped the horse and focused my attention to hear above my nervous breaths. It was faint, but I heard German whispers among the trees along the other side. I couldn't make out exactly what they were saying, but

I could tell that the sounds started to fade as the German soldiers walked away from the ravine and down the slope into the dark forest. I waited for several minutes on my horse in still silence. Exhaling, I loosened the reins and prodded the horse forward.

I continued on high alert, with my right hand firmly holding my pistol and left hand clutching the reins. The horse approached a bend and suddenly a shadow emerged.

"*Stoi ne smecte* (Don't move)," ordered the shadow.

I froze. The command was in Russian, but there were many German collaborators who would gladly turn a Soviet soldier into a German—or worse, discover I was a Jew. The shadow approached my horse slowly and wrapped one hand around the reins while keeping the other hovering over his sidearm. "Let go of the reins," the voice instructed.

I heard people rustle leaves around me and could feel their weapons trained on me. My right hand rested on the butt of my pistol, and my left hand still held the reins tight. The package was enclosed, secure in a satchel across my chest. My heartbeat filled my ears, making it hard to hear or think. My fear of capture and torture exceeded fear of death. Feeling the pistol in my hand, I considered shooting myself before allowing them to disarm me. I breathed heavily, the moment seemingly lasting an eternity. It would be impossible either to flee or fight through this situation; I would certainly be shot in an instant. Then again, it was also possible that I was in the right place. The shadow was no help, refusing to let me know whether I had arrived at the secret base or fallen into enemy hands. Still without identifying itself, the voice repeated the command. "Let go of the reins."

I clutched my pistol, keeping my index finger near the trigger, and let go of the reins. The shadow clicked his tongue and guided the horse forward. The people hiding in the brush emerged, and their silhouettes escorted me toward a dim light in the distance. I was extremely nervous, expecting to be dragged off to some miserable fate at any moment.

The man stopped the horse outside of a tent and ordered me to get down. Clutching my pistol, I eased off the horse, alert and apprehensive. I never got a clear look at any of the men who guided me to this point. As soon as I stood in front of the tent, the men dispersed. The horse was eased away, someone whispering words of approval into the horse's ear.

The tent opened, spilling light out onto the dirt. Squinting, I could see a small group of uniformed Soviet officers standing over a small table. I exhaled in relief. A pleasant officer welcomed me in, commending me for successfully riding the horse to the base camp. Still nervous from the experience, I fumbled through my pouch and handed a sealed package to the commanding officer.

The officer looked at me and asked if I was alright. I was pale, and my hands were shaking. Slowly realizing that everything was fine, I began to calm down and let out a nervous laugh. "I thought...I mean, I wasn't sure..." I stammered. "I thought I fell into German hands. So, I am in the correct place?" I searched the faces of the officers in the room for confirmation. The officers paused, and then roared with laughter. They teased me mercilessly as the commander brought out a few shots of vodka to settle my nerves and toast a good laugh.

I didn't remain at the camp long. Soon after delivering the package and downing a few shots, I departed to try and make it back before sunrise. The same horse was waiting to take me back to my camp. I hopped on much more confidently than before and rode off.

The horse continued to make his way deftly through the woods as I peered between the shadows of early light to be sure that the road was safe. The chirping birds and rustle of the critters echoed throughout the forest; I wouldn't have been able to hear those Germans whispering over the forest noise. Halfway into the ride, the predawn light revealed the narrow path, and I could make out the silhouettes of trees.

Suddenly, there was an explosion. Mortar fire. My horse reared up and I jumped off. I couldn't tell which direction the fire was coming from, but shells were being volleyed back and forth across the forest, and I was in the middle. I held onto the horse's reins and ran next to him for cover. Desperately trying to keep up with the horse, I jumped logs and rocks, trying to maintain my balance as I sprinted with every fiber in my being. I eventually made it to the clearing where my base was visible. An officer noticed me emerge from the forest and waved me over to the stable. Panting, I handed him the reins and stumbled away to recover.

After catching my breath, I reported to the Colonel to inform him of the successful mission. He was pleased to hear it but was focused on the firefight with the Germans. The Colonel reached for a sheet of paper and handed it to me while continuing to issue orders to other officers. He quickly turned to me and said that I would need to follow the orders right away.

My orders: escort a sergeant to the front lines—a *shtrafbat* order. An order of this kind for a higher-ranking soldier was usually a punishment for criminal or deviant behavior. Such an order was a near-certain death sentence since casualties on the front lines were high. I went to the barracks to retrieve the soldier. There was a guard watching over him. It was only when I stood in front of the soldier and opened the paper to read the order that I realized my dilemma.

"Viktor Aleyivich," I said. The man looked up with sullen eyes. "I have orders for you; we will depart soon." The man nodded. I needed a moment to consider this situation. The soldier was obviously Jewish. I read my orders again: Escort the soldier to front lines and shoot him if he tries to escape. I could not bear to personally deliver a fellow Jew to a near-certain death. Plus, I was exhausted from the harrowing events of the night before.

Wearily, I returned to the Colonel. "I have reviewed the orders," I said. "Due to fatigue and exhaustion from my previous mission, I request to be excused from this assignment."

The Colonel was busy holding multiple conversations. He didn't even fully consider my request. Unmoved, he waved me off and said, "Sleep when you get back."

Grimly, I made my way back to the barracks and met the stare of the Jewish soldier. Sympathetic to the Jewish soldier's predicament, I sat across from him. "I don't want to have to take you to the front line," I said. He nodded again. "I also have orders to shoot you if you try to escape." I stood and paced to control my emotions. "I don't know why you are ordered to the front, and I'm sorry that we are in the situation, but I have to follow these orders." Then I asked in Yiddish, "*Fursteisht*? (Understand?)"

The soldier smiled faintly. "I'll make it easy for you," he assured me. "I promise. I won't try to escape."

I folded the paper away. "Then, let's go," I said. He walked in front of me toward a waiting car before which stood a driver and a female logistics supervisor. I shared the orders with the woman, who scanned the sheet and then provided the driver with instructions. The driver was not to know the specifics of the journey but followed the instructions the logistics supervisor provided. After several hours, we reached the front. The soldier and I parted, wishing each other well.

On the ride back, I thought more about my dilemma. There were Jews who served in the Russian army, but rarely was a word spoken openly about our religion or heritage. Only in the shadows did we whisper about the fate of our people—and rumors about ghettos and mass murders were becoming more frequent and increasingly detailed. Recalling years of Soviet pogroms and anti-Semitism, we, as Jews, had no illusions about our situation: Russians sacrificed themselves for national preservation; Jews marched alongside for ethnic survival. It had pained me to escort Viktor to the front, and I wished there was some way I could have avoided it. Then again, maybe he'd done something terrible and deserved the sentence. I would never know. I pursued these thoughts for a while until the rhythmic ride back from the front lulled me sleep.

Chapter 16:
Bessarabia

"Heil Hitler...you son of a bitch...Heil Hitler," spat the Russian soldiers at the German POWs. Columns of German POWs marched under Russian command, forced to rebuild the cities they had destroyed. The Soviets were merciless on these enemies. Germans died from disease, hunger, and fatigue. We couldn't care less. These people were responsible for devastating countless lives, so their only remaining value was to repair what they'd broken—and if it cost them their lives, so be it.

The Germans believed that, as POWs, they would return to their homes and therefore surrendered when captured. The Ukrainian resistance fighters, on the other hand, would not accept the fate of POWs. A fight with them was to the death. The Ukrainians that had sided with the Germans had nowhere else to go; it was either fight the Soviets for national self-determination or die trying. Pockets of these groups took the longest to eradicate, but eventually they too succumbed to the Western advance.

If one didn't know better, one might think that the Soviets occupied the moral high ground in the war—that they would protect the innocent. But I knew better. They weren't much better than the Germans they fought. Pogroms and anti-Semitism proved it. It was in Yasha, Bessarabia, where I witnessed a perfect example of this.

It was sometime in late 1944. I could hardly believe my eyes, but in the center of the town stood a middle-aged Jewish man, grinning broadly and expressing his gratitude to any Russian soldier that would listen. The meek Jew gained the attention of a few Russian soldiers by bringing them a pack of matches so they could smoke. Smug disdain was written all over their faces; they were disgusted with this poor man.

Oblivious to their body language, the Jew struggled to express himself in Russian, explaining that he was Romanian and was grateful to the soldiers for liberating him. The Jew said that the Germans are soulless and evil, and that the Russians are "*kulturish*"—more cultured as a people. Laughing at the Jew, the Russian pushed him so hard that he fell. The soldier then exposed his genitals, and, imitating a Yiddish dialect, said, "*A chueyish kulturish!*" The Russians picked up the matches and walked away, laughing and mocking the Jew.

Dumbfounded, the Jew just sat there in the mud, confused about what had just happened. Feeling bad for the man, I walked over and helped him up. I didn't have the heart to tell him that *chuey* in Russian meant penis and that the soldiers couldn't care less about this Jew. He gave me an awkward smile and thanked me in Russian, but the joy in his face was gone. Embarrassed, he looked down and started to walk away, when I asked him in Yiddish, "*Vi file idn zenen linx in rumenye?* (How many Jews are left in Romania?)"

The Jew froze and looked at me in astonishment. He introduced himself as Sholom Rodan, eagerly shaking my hand. He bombarded me with questions. How had I come to be a soldier in the Red Army? Where was I from? Were there many Jews in the army? Finally recognizing that I hadn't responded, he apologized for his exuberance and invited me to meet a few other Jewish civilians who had managed to evade German capture.

I walked with him to a dilapidated shack where a handful of gaunt Jewish men sat absently staring at the commotion of the liberating Red Army moving through their town. As I strode in with Sholom, the men noticed my uniform and slowly pulled themselves up to stand at attention. I smiled humbly, waving my hand for them to sit and rest. Sholom excitedly explained to the men that I was a Polish

Jew who ended up in the Red Army. Collectively, they looked up and nodded in approval. Sholom asked if the men would share what they knew about the Jews of Romania.

One of the men motioned for me to sit. In a faint voice, the man said he was Josef from Bessarabia and had a young family: a daughter and a newborn son. Josef was a tailor. He was a young man, but by the look of him, the war had aged him by decades. He operated a small but growing business, earning a reputation for his quality work. A few families had managed to leave Josef's town prior to 1941 but most had remained, believing that Romania would be protected from German invasion by Soviet forces. As I listened to Josef describe the situation before 1941, I immediately thought of Dubno. It was the same everywhere.

In June 1941, Germany invaded Romania. Josef said that there was no time to prepare or respond to the attack. Tanks, trucks, and soldiers stormed across the border and into the cities with little to no resistance. Many young men fled east into the USSR, but with a young family, he had judged it better to hide and stay out of the way of the gunfire. Each day and night was a terror—planes bombing, tanks shelling, people running. Whatever Soviet military presence had existed in Bessarabia dissipated quickly. Soldiers either retreated or were killed, their dead bodies lying in roads and on fields. After the initial German onslaught, the Romanians led many of the attacks against the Jews. It was hard to believe what Josef had witnessed. Germans sat on their hands casually chatting as Romanian soldiers and civilians savagely attacked innocent Jews. Listening to this horror, I thought to myself, *This is what must have happened in Dubno.*

Voice cracking, fighting through tears, Josef continued his story. Gunshots and screams filled the streets as women were molested and killed, men summarily shot at random. Josef hid with other Jews in the cellar of an old factory, hoping to protect his children. After several days of constant killing, the Germans instructed the Romanians to round up Jews in large groups. At first it seemed that the worst was over, since the gunshots and screams had quieted down.

They came door to door, ordering Jews out at gunpoint but not firing a shot. The Jews were herded together by the thousands— men, women and children trembling in fear. It was impossible to see through the crowds. Josef and his family desperately tried to stay together as they were hurried to an open square. A large group of Jews filled the square, nervous and frightened. Everyone stood around with questioning looks, hoping to understand what they should be doing. Josef held his wife and children, trying to console them. Then one gunshot cracked through the air, and the entire mass of Jews froze. There were Romanians and Germans standing on trucks encircling the square, many smirking, all leveling machine guns at the crowd of frightened civilians. "Fire!" came the German command, sending a torrent of bullets into the helpless crowd.

Josef sobbed as he described how his wife and children were murdered. Limbs flailed in all directions, crushing the crowd inward. Josef's wife was shot and died instantly. Josef moved to grab his infant son from her falling arms but was crushed by the mangled bodies, pinning him to the ground. Josef reached desperately for his children, his young daughter screaming at the sight of her dead mother. The baby fell to the ground, smothered under a pile of bloody clothes. Josef clawed to reach them but could not move. Writhing, he managed to grab his daughter's hand. Before he could say anything to her, she was shot in the chest and fell lifeless. Shielded by bodies, Josef miraculously remained alive, trapped in a mass of murdered Jews. Horrific screams echoed in the square, but what stayed with Josef was the laughter. The Germans and Romanians laughed as they murdered.

When the artillery fire stopped, moans and pleas rose from the pile of the dead. Josef and others that survived the attack managed to crawl out and escape in the night. He survived in the woods with a few Jews from Bukovina, who had survived similar massacres. Josef said that he observed thousands of Jews march east toward Ukraine; many would die from starvation, disease, or murder along the way.

I listened, dumbfounded. I'd witnessed plenty of death in combat and by starvation. War was awful—but again I struggled to comprehend the scale of civilian suffering and death and the evil that could drive people to behave this way. I grieved with Josef. Once again, I could not help but think about Dubno and my family. I boiled with rage; I wanted every last German dead. Romania had a Jewish population of 757,000 before World War II. In total, approximately 400,000 Jews, including the Jews of Transnistria, were murdered in Romanian-controlled areas under the wartime dictatorship of Ion Antonescu.[xiv]

Chapter 17:
Shabbat in Romania

I spent the next few weeks absently working with other Red Army soldiers picking over German equipment and supplies discarded during their hasty retreat. We made our way across Romania toward the Tisa River, preparing for the Battle of Debrecen. We all started to believe that victory was possible. Despite the hope, I could not help but think about Josef's story; the images of the massacre burned into my mind. My thoughts constantly drifted back to Dubno, envisioning the synagogue, the soccer fields, and the open square of the marketplace. Was my family killed in the same way? Aaron's letter didn't specify. Then again, Josef had managed to survive. Maybe my family had as well. Perhaps they were struggling for survival in the forest, waiting for me to find them?

One night, after completing a mission outside of Arad, not far from the Hungarian border, I passed some homes that were still intact and noticed in one house a pair of lit candles in the window. I thought aloud, "It must be Shabbos..." Watching the candles flicker, I felt a profound longing and sadness, remembering Shabbat evenings at home and the time I spent with family and friends. I envisioned my mother and sister covering their eyes, reciting the traditional prayer welcoming the Sabbath Queen, my brother and I standing on either side of our father as he held the cup of wine and sang the Kiddush prayer. My eyes welled up recalling how my parents pulled us together and bestowed the blessing over children upon us. Now, I would never spend another Shabbat with my family. It was so hard to accept.

Drawn irresistibly to the candlelight in the window, I carefully approached. It was a typical rural village house, unassuming and quaint. A fire crackled into the chimney, sending a rising stream of smoke into the night sky. I paused, looking around to see if anyone was watching me. If I'd seen anyone else, I probably would have continued on my way back to the base, avoiding the house altogether. But there was no one in sight. Save for the odd rustle of fallen leaves or the sounds of livestock from neighboring farms, the village was quiet. So, I edged closer to the house, standing across from the door.

I suddenly felt very uncomfortable. I wasn't sure what I would say to the people who answered the door: I missed my home? What if they weren't Jewish? What if it was some crazy trap? Despite the second-guessing, I gently knocked on the door. It took only a few moments before I heard the shuffling inside of someone coming to the door, but I was already backing away, worried I'd made a mistake. Then the door opened, revealing an older Jewish couple that could have easily fit in to the Dubno community.

"*Yiddin* (Jews)?" I asked uncertainly. The old woman clutched the man, her eyes searching me—clearly nervous when she noticed my PPSh. Her eyes darted past me to look for other soldiers. The man paused, equally worried about the consequences of his answer. Still apprehensive about the soldier standing in front of him, the old man threaded his fingers through his beard, twirling the end of the hair in his fingertips, and hesitantly nodded yes.

I smiled, relieved. I leaned in to whisper, "I am a Polish Jew." I stumbled over my next words, unburdening myself of years of anxiety, eager to share with someone—anyone—how far I had come. I explained how I'd come to be a refugee and been conscripted into the Russian army. I don't know why, but I went on to tell of my encounter with Sholom and Josef from Romania, noting that these were the first civilian Jews I'd met since Kalinovka. As I babbled on their doorstep about how great it was to see the Shabbos candles, the couple ushered me in, peeking into the darkness, hoping to avoid any unwelcome attention.

They were clearly overwhelmed to see a Jewish solider stammering on their doorstep but were equally welcoming and hospitable. They smiled and nodded as I rambled on about myself and how grateful I was to see Jews that had survived. Eventually, when I paused for a breath, the old man placed a supportive hand on my shoulder, giving me a squeeze and pat, letting me know I was welcome in his home. "Gut Shabbos, I am Chaim Mayer, and this is my wife Rivka," he said.

"Gut Shabbos," I responded. "I am Vladimir Nuss—" I caught myself. I realized I hadn't used my true name in years. "I am Wolf Kogul, from Dubno." It felt liberating to use my name, to be free from the Soviet military structure—to be Jewish again.

"Nu Wolf, would you like to spend the Sabbath with us?" Chaim asked.

I had completed my mission. If I was late by one more day, no one would mind, least of all the Colonel—especially if I managed to bring with me some trinket for one of his pretty ladies. I nodded. "I would be honored to spend the Sabbath with you."

"Good," Chaim responded. "We will go to the synagogue in the morning."

My eyes widened. "Synagogue? There are other Jews?"

"Yes," he responded. "A small group of Jews survived, and our synagogue is damaged, but we recently are able to get together quietly and complete a short service in the mornings. With you, we will have a *minyan.*" I was stunned, but I beamed—honored to be the tenth man.

Even though the couple had already recited blessings, they repeated the prayers over the candles for my benefit, welcoming the Sabbath for me. They even had some hard bread, which I gratefully devoured. We sat in their living room, on comfortable chairs with simple, cushioned seats. There were books everywhere—in stacks, on shelves—and papers piled randomly. It looked more like a rabbinical study than a house.

Chaim looked at me, uncertain how to begin a conversation with a fellow Jew who sat with a PPSh on his lap. He patted my knee. "It is good to see a Jew fighting the Nazi evil," he began. Chaim opened his mouth to say something but stopped himself. There was a distant look in his eyes, as though he was imagining himself somewhere else. G-d knows what nightmares he was reliving in his mind. A moment later, he cleared his throat. "Most Jews never had a chance to defend themselves," he said, his voice trailing off.

I sighed sympathetically, telling them that I really didn't have much of a choice. It was really just luck that I managed to survive and end up in the Soviet army—and I wasn't even sure how lucky I was to be in the army. Chaim nodded in agreement—but I detected a quiver in his chin as he pursed his lips to keep his composure. Rivka patted Chaim's back, consoling him. She glanced at the gun in my lap, still nervous. Chaim straightened his back, fighting back the emotion which had seized him so suddenly.

I set the gun down on the floor between my legs, which seemed to put Rivka slightly more at ease. I leaned in and looked at both of them. I was amazed by how this couple managed to survive when so many young, able-bodied men fell so quickly. "In all the cities we liberated," I said, breaking the silence, "I never came across any civilian Jews. Across all of the Caucasus and the Ukraine, Jewish life was erased. At first, I thought it was because of the Soviet order to burn towns. Then I thought it was because of the Soviet fighting with the Germans. But then I realized it wasn't just destruction from war; it felt like something else. I started to hear the stories of mass murders and mass graves. And then I met Josef, a Romanian Jew who told me the most awful story about a murder in his town square." The couple nodded knowingly. "How did you manage to survive?" I blurted out.

The couple smiled grimly at each other, Rivka's eyes welling up. "The pogroms under Antonescu were terrible," Chaim began. "Our son, Moshe, was studying to become a rabbi and wanted to open a synagogue in the village areas to offer Jews outside the city center a place to worship." Rivka, unable to listen to the story, rose and went to the kitchen to boil water. "We were registered in the city center, where we had lived our entire lives. It was only after Moshe and his wife, Leah, had their firstborn—Menachem, after my father—that Rivka and I left the city center to join them in the village to help Leah with the boy as they built their *shul*." Shaking slightly, Chaim, said, "You see, Wolf, it was because we were registered in the city center that there was no record of us here."

My eyes drifted around the room slowly—the books, pages of writings, the scholarly desk. I was beginning to understand, with a growing sense of foreboding, that the house I was in was not the old couple's home but that of their son.

"We were accustomed to the pogroms, as miserable as they were," Chaim continued. "The Romanians usually destroyed property, and only occasionally was someone seriously injured or worse. But after 1939, the situation deteriorated. We felt it would be better to be in the villages far outside the city center and away from the focus of Romanian—and German—eyes. Several families decided to leave, those with relatives in other lands. But where could we go? Our family was here. We had only one son, and he had just begun a family of his own. So, we decided to stay with him and, G-d willing, help him raise more children." Chaim's voice cracked as he fought back tears.

"When the war broke out," Chaim went on, "Antonescu aligned with Hitler, leaving all of the Jews defenseless. Those that managed to flee the city center and ran through our village warned us to run for our lives—the Romanians were killing Jews indiscriminately. We couldn't believe it. And where could we go? We thought it would be safer to stay and hide than run in the open. There is a cellar underneath this house, for storing food in the winter. Moshe begged us to hide in there, reasoning that there was no record of us living at this house. On the day that the Germans entered this village, Moshe's last words to us were, 'Please keep the Sabbath.' He kissed us both, hid us in the cellar with a week's worth of food, and concealed the cellar door with his desk and books."

Chaim looked at me with grave emphasis. "Wolf," he said, "I can't tell you I believe in G-d anymore, but my son would have wanted me to believe. So, I keep the Sabbath in his honor." I turned cold, casting my eyes down at the floor.

"The first night in the cellar was awful," Chaim recounted. "My poor Rivka—she worried the entire night, listening to Moshe moving furniture and books around, trying to protect his parents." His voice trailing off, Chaim said, "It should have been me protecting them." He was openly sobbing now, wiping the tears on his sleeve.

"The next morning," Chaim resumed, "we heard the thunder of trucks and tanks entering the village. Romanian and German soldiers were shouting, dogs were barking. It was difficult to hear what they were saying since the sounds were muffled in the cellar. We heard screams in the distance, but again, it was difficult to understand what was happening above us. We were able to hear Leah singing to the baby—a lullaby, just like the ones that Rivka sang to Moshe. The tension was inescapable. Each minute was excruciating. The rumbles of the trucks grew louder, and a metallic screech split the air outside the house as the trucks stopped somewhere near. We could hear German. Suddenly, there was a thunderous bang on the door, nearly rattling the door off its hinges. Activity in the house froze, and the banging resumed again. The poor baby cried, wailing from the violent sounds. Footsteps paced toward the door, and there was an exchange of words. Someone stated in Romanian Moshe and Leah's names. Rivka was in knots, and I was holding her to keep her quiet. It was unbearable: I was helpless and, like a blind man, suffered to only hear the torment above. The discussion at the door did not last long. It concluded abruptly with the sound of a gunshot. There was no warning, nothing to prepare us: just one single shot and the thud that followed. Rivka gasped, and I was forced to hold her down with my hand over her mouth, practically gagging her. Leah screamed, and I knew that my son was dead. She screamed and screamed, and the baby wailed uncontrollably. And then there were a series of gunshots tearing through the house, sending bullets through the floor." With my eyes cast down, I noticed the torn floorboards and bullet holes.

"Leah didn't cry anymore," Chaim said. "And neither did the baby." Rivka was sobbing in the kitchen. Chaim was pulling on his hair in agony. This was the first time they'd ever shared their story. They'd never had the opportunity to let go of the guilt. "Rivka and I remained paralyzed in that cellar," Chaim continued. "Our only family murdered above us. And we are now alive only because of our son." Chaim sat crying on his sofa as I sat helplessly slouched in the chair with my hands in my lap.

After a few moments of silent anguish, the words just escaped my lips. "*Yitgadal, v'yitkadash...*" I hadn't spoken those words in years. I wasn't sure if I even believed anymore myself, after everything that I'd been through. I recited the Mourner's Kaddish instinctively, at first to console the grieving couple, but as the words left my mouth, I began to think about my own loss. Of the family I would not see and of the countless many I saw murdered. I pushed the thought of my loss aside; I didn't have time for my pain. Chaim joined in the Kaddish, weeping. We sat there together, grieving. Chaim leaned over and gave me a thankful pat on the knee.

Chaim wiped the tears from his eyes and looked at me with a

vulnerable smile. "We remained in the cellar for two weeks, rationing the food, silently crying daily," he said. "The gunshots and screams continued for several more days after...and then the trucks drove away. We didn't dare leave the cellar until it was completely quiet. When we ran out of food, we had no choice. The village was silent, abandoned for several days. The soldiers had moved on with their attacks, and this small village wasn't even worth them leaving behind any presence. In the days and weeks that followed, a handful of other Jews appeared—those who managed to hide and avoid the murders. The blood of our children remained on our floor; several months passed before we could bring ourselves to clean it. There are only a few dozen survivors in this village. We are frozen in this place—too afraid to leave. We wouldn't even know where to go. We have no rabbi; my son is gone. So, in his honor, we keep the Sabbath, and a few of the other men agree to pray with us."

I leaned in toward Chaim and told him how sorry I was for his loss. He nodded appreciatively, then stood. "Thank you for saying Kaddish," he said. "You've honored my family." I rose to meet him, searching for words of comfort. He hugged me, as though he was holding his son, and prayed for my safety.

Chaim and Rivka escorted me to a guest room, and after bidding me goodnight, they closed the door. I was overwhelmed—physically exhausted from the mission but mentally depleted from listening to Chaim. I felt awful for them. Parents should not outlive their children.

I settled into an overstuffed featherbed. I had forgotten how wonderfully soft a bed like this could be. The fluffy sheets enveloped my limbs and caressed my cheek. I exhaled, expecting I would be able to drift away easily. But no matter which way I turned, I could not get comfortable. It was ironic: This was the first proper bed I'd had in years, and I couldn't fall asleep. I gave up trying. I moved to the hard floor, pulled my jacket over my head, and went to sleep.

Chaim and Rivka awoke early in the morning to find me sleeping on the floor with my jacket draped over me. Noticing the expression of confusion on their faces, I explained that the bed was too soft and that I was not accustomed to such comfort. They sighed in understanding.

I walked with the couple to a small, dilapidated building that served as the local synagogue. A dozen or so Jews were praying there. They looked at me awkwardly because of the gun strapped over my shoulder. Hearing the prayers I'd recited countless times before, I stood among the devoted Jews with more ambivalence than reverence. By now, I had ceased to believe in G-d, although my Jewish identity remained steadfast. I was honored to serve as the tenth man in the *minyan*, but I can't say I was particularly present; my mind repeatedly wandered.

After returning from services, Chaim, Rivka and I sat and drank a cup of tea together. They only had large mugs the size of soup bowls. They filled the water nearly to the brim and then added a little milk. We sipped our tea slowly, careful not to spill. I asked the couple about their plans. They shrugged and said that when the war was over, they would dedicate themselves to their son's cause: supporting Jewish communities in small villages. Finishing my large bowl of tea, I thanked them for their generosity and left. I never forgot their hospitality, and I have continued to drink my tea from a large bowl filled to the very top ever since.

Nearly a year had passed since I'd learned that my family had been murdered by the Germans. The first Shabbat I was able to observe since then made me long for home. Leaving the old couple's house, I recalled how my mother generously hosted strangers and cared for the poor. The words in Aaron's letter reverberated in my mind, but I couldn't blindly accept that my entire family had been killed. Josef had survived. Chaim, Rivka, and a few other Jews from this village had survived. Maybe some of my family members were in hiding too. I could not wait any longer; I needed to go to Dubno and see for myself.

Chapter 18:
Return to Dubno

"I'm going to Dubno," I informed the Colonel. As usual, he was poring over maps, planning the next series of missions. He looked up at me. Seeing the determination in my eyes, he stroked his chin and paused to think. Filling the silence, I continued, "Dubno was liberated earlier this year, and I must go to find out any information I can about my family."

The Colonel stood, paced, and eyed me carefully. Suddenly, I realized that I had never challenged the Colonel or spoken to him in anything other than a deferential tone. I hoped that my years of loyal service and accomplishment would sway him, but maybe I was wrong. Still, I would not accept anything other than time off to go to Dubno.

He unrolled a map of the region and pointed to several areas with red-striped markings. "The Germans are still there, not far outside Dubno," he said. I was relieved that he took me seriously and didn't summarily send me to a *shtrafbat*.

"At the rate the Germans are retreating, by the time I arrive, the Germans will be gone," I countered.

The Colonel was tapping the maps and surveying the environment again. He turned to me and gave me a long, understanding look. "Okay, Volodya, you have two weeks," he said. He directed me to speak with the office and supplies manager in order to surrender my pistol, since these were in limited supply.

The manager warned of the threat of criminals and suggested I take my PPSh for protection. I was sick and tired of this damn war. I was on my way to see about my family. I was on my way home for the first time since I left. I couldn't think clearly. I scarcely paid attention to the manager's words. I was exhausted. I didn't want anything else to do with guns or war. So, I walked away unarmed.

My military ID granted me access on any military transport, and after several days of hitching rides on convoys, I boarded an early morning train to Dubno. The ride was slow and long, and as I finally neared Dubno in the slanting afternoon sun, my numbness from the war left me, and the somber reality of what was left of home began to sink in. As the train approached the station, I was jarred from my ruminations by the crackling of gunfire—the station was engulfed in resistance battle. I couldn't tell who was shooting at whom. Unarmed and alone, my only asset was my knowledge of the station I knew so well as a child. I jumped off the train and hid in an underground chamber where I waited out the firefight.

The raging afternoon firefight gradually subsided throughout the evening, and as the moonlit sky became the only source of light, the last stray shots ceased. Sensing the battle was over, I emerged from my hiding place and made my way over the platform, out of the station, and into the shadowy streets of a largely abandoned Dubno. The road to the city center was roughly a mile, but the eerie stillness of the midnight air and my crunching steps on a rubble path made the distance seem much farther. Wandering aimlessly through the deserted town, I was lost: directionless, numb, sad, alone.

I noticed an unassuming house emitting a faint glow from a mostly covered window. Uncertain of who might answer, I gently knocked on the door. A moment later, a tired and worn older man opened the door. Adjusting my eyes to the light, I recognized the man—a Jewish shopkeeper who was well-respected in the community. Gladdened to see a familiar face, I whispered, "I am Wolf Kogul, from Dubno." Aaron Grossberg, who coincidentally was inside the house, was awakened by the knocking and slowly made his way to see what was going on.

Aaron arrived at the door, rubbing the sleep from his eyes. Focusing on my face, he clasped his hands. "Oy! Wolf!" he exclaimed. "Thank G-d you are alive! Come in, come in."

Aaron's excited voice woke the rest of the house. Other relatives and neighbors were soon huddled together in the home and welcomed me in. I could not believe what I was seeing. So many of my relatives alive! I hugged and kissed everyone. Their faces became a swirling blur, and I was overcome with emotion. It was a moment of intoxicating jubilation—they survived! Somehow, against all odds, my family made it!

My heart pounded as I tried to refocus my eyes on the faces in the room. I kept searching and searching but didn't spot the faces of my mother, my father, my sister, my brother. I had forgotten the letter I'd received nearly a year earlier. Giddy, nervous, I kept smiling. It was then that the words just leapt out of my mouth. "Where is my Mom?" I asked, fully expecting that she would miraculously appear.

A hush blanketed the room and everyone lowered their heads, looking for answers on the floor. Confused, my eyes darted around the fallen faces, searching for a response. The air was sucked out of the room. I couldn't understand why everyone had turned so somber. It was Aaron who first raised his eyes toward mine and approached me slowly. His sad, consoling eyes answered my question. I started to nod my head even before he asked, "Did you receive the letter I sent?" His words trailed off. The dark reality swallowed my fleeting euphoria. Everything was awful again. Everyone in the room separated and sat down. I just stood there. I sank into silence, feeling the gravity of the sadness weighing us all down. No more words were spoken. Everyone retired to their internal grief and slept.

The following morning, I woke early after a troubled sleep and wandered through the town. The streets and homes and shops and trees that were once so familiar were disfigured and paralyzed. The life that once pulsed through this town was gone, showing no sign of returning. The Germans murdered well; I hated them and wanted every last one of them dead.

After an hour of pacing, seeking, hoping, I found myself on a familiar street. The homes were badly damaged and in disrepair. As I passed them, I could hardly believe that this was the same street on which I grew up, on which I played as a child, on which I said my last goodbye to my family. And there it was. Three years before, I stood in the doorway and promised to be back soon. Three years before, my mother assured me that asking for food was nothing to be ashamed of. Three years before, I waved off my younger brother when he begged to come with me, the words still ringing in my mind: "*Nameh ana rameh.*" Three years. A lifetime.

I stood before the house in which I was born and raised—my home. From the outside, the house seemed abandoned, so I walked in somberly. I stepped into the living room and looked down the hallway of the barren house. The pictures and ornaments that once adorned my Jewish home were gone. The revered picture of Sholem Aleichem that hung above the mantelpiece was gone. Samovar gone. Nothing was left except the shell of a wooden house. It was an uncomfortable feeling being a stranger in your own home. I just stood there, still, in the middle of the house, hoping to connect to something. Memories, like ghosts, flickered in the lifeless rooms. It's gone, I sighed and continued to the rear of the house.

I opened the door to my bedroom and was shocked to see a woman cradling a small child. I nearly roared, "Who the hell are you and what are you doing in my house?" But I didn't say a word. I just stood there, paralyzed, angry. She was equally surprised. Clutching her child nervously, she stupidly stammered that her husband was out fighting the Russians. I guess she didn't know what a Russian uniform looked like. Here was the wife of a man who was out fighting my army, killing Jews! And these bastards stole my house! I suppose it's a good thing that I didn't have the PPSh with me; I might have gunned them down right then and there. But I didn't. I could tell the woman was anxious and worried about what I would do to her. *We weren't the ones degrading and raping and torturing and murdering innocent women and children*, I thought to myself. *It was you who were doing that to us.* I retraced my steps through the house and exited the front door, out through the small yard, and onto the street. Helpless, I turned and looked into my stolen home; hopeless, I wept and walked away.

I left my house angry and confused. I needed to have some answers about what happened here; in retrospect, I wish I'd never received them. I spent the remaining few days in Dubno with Aaron, learning about what had happened to the Jews of Dubno, my family, relatives, and friends. Aaron explained as best he could, describing the initial assault by the Germans, the heinous murders by the Ukrainians, and then, ultimately, the mass executions. Frustrated by what appeared to be a Jewish capitulation to the Germans, I asked contemptuously, "Why didn't the Jews fight back? They realized their fate; better to fight and die rather than be slaughtered." Aaron sighed and related a story.

It happened well after most of the Jews of Dubno had been murdered. "Several dozen Jews remained hiding in the ghetto," Aaron began. "Dubno was largely destroyed. One morning, an SS officer charged, gun in hand, to the center of the ghetto and called out to the hiding Jews. He proclaimed that he had no intention of causing them further harm and just wanted to speak with them—this was, of course, before the final mass execution of the remaining Jews. His repeated pleas were received with skepticism, but eventually, seeing the inevitability of the situation, the Jews slowly emerged from their hiding places and stood shabbily before the armed German soldiers.

"Among the Jews, there was one man, Menachem, who was a large and imposing figure. Despite his weathered appearance, it was obvious that in his prime he was a man of formidable strength. In fact, before the war broke out, Menachem was known to have lifted a small horse on his back in order to help the hurt animal receive medical assistance. The SS officer immediately noticed Menachem and approached him. The towering Jew stared blankly at the ground with defeated eyes. The SS officer drew his pistol and thrust it into Menachem's fleshy hand. The SS officer then challenged Menachem to shoot him. It was unclear what had motivated the SS officer, but some suspected that he must have been overcome by guilt. Menachem felt the cold pistol in his hand and slowly lifted his head. He quietly said, 'I know that I can pull this trigger and kill you, but I was not raised to kill.' Menachem then dropped the gun on the floor. His spoken words sent a chill through the SS officer, who in disgust began cursing the Jews. He snatched his pistol, clubbed Menachem, and marched off."

Aaron stared off absently, leaving me to absorb the story. I lit a cigarette, held in the smoke, and then exhaled with a slow nod. Passing the cigarette to Aaron, I thought of Menachem. No, we were not raised to kill. But the war had changed me.

"So, tell me more," I beseeched Aaron. "What happened to my family?" Aaron was visibly uncomfortable. He said he felt guilty to survive when so many had died. He felt equally terrible to have to tell me what happened to my family. "Your father and brother were killed when the Germans first entered Dubno," Aaron began slowly. I knew their fate, but the words stabbed my gut, twisting the pain to my core. Again, my brother's words came back to me. *Nameh ana rameh.*

"About your sister..." Aaron resumed. "Before the Germans established the ghetto, your father told several of us about where Sarah was located—just in case a family member would survive the war."

"She was with Mudrik, right?" I asked, half hoping that somehow she was still alive.

Walking back to Aaron's home, Aaron confirmed that Sarah was supposed to be kept safe with a Ukrainian family. He even knew that my father had done some business with Mudrik and that Mudrik had a daughter that attended school with Sarah. Aaron said that Mudrik had in fact protected Sarah and kept the material goods my father had bartered in exchange. Sarah was apparently kept safe for quite some time, but after Mudrik's daughter learned to sew sufficiently, she, for whatever reason, informed Ukrainian or German officers about Sarah. Sarah's fate was uncertain, as there were no further accounts of what happened to her. When Aaron received my letter from the Soviet front, indicating that I was alive, he visited Mudrik to check on Sarah and told him of my status.

Upon seeing Aaron, Mudrik turned pale. He didn't even properly invite Aaron inside. Rather, he staggered backward, leaving the door open for Aaron to enter. Mudrik paced nervously, babbling randomly about the war and the toll it took on his wife's health. "What could I do?" Mudrik shouted to the empty space in his living room. Mudrik glanced at Aaron and mumbled, "She was taken." He kept mumbling it over and over again, louder each time until Aaron was compelled to close the door behind him for fear of being overheard by people out in the street.

Mudrik clearly felt guilty. Aaron just looked at him with sad bewilderment, uncertain whether it was safe for him to remain with a man so unstable. Mudrik continued to pace around the room, nervously stammering that he wouldn't keep any of the belongings, that he would turn them all over to the NKVD. Suddenly, Mudrik's remorse turned to defiant rage. "I took an enormous risk, you know!" he shouted, raising a clenched fist. "My family could have been killed!" Mudrik was furious now. Aaron never said a word; he just sighed and backed away toward the door. "Get out!" Mudrik screamed. "Never come back here! If you ever mention anything to anyone, I will deny that I ever protected her!" With Mudrik fuming, Aaron quickly departed.

I was numb. The discussion my father and Mudrik had in our house replayed in my mind; their argument, their agreement. My thoughts then turned to Sarah. She'd been so worried about Natasha. Sarah knew. She knew she couldn't trust Natasha. I felt so helpless. So angry.

Entering Aaron's house, Aaron interrupted my thoughts as he

cleared his throat. "You never responded to my letter," he said. Refocusing, I looked at him, confused. "You never responded to my letter," he repeated. Suddenly I realized. I was going to explain how I was so demoralized to read about the death of my family, how the demands of war consumed every moment. But I didn't have a chance. "We thought you were killed," Aaron said. I nodded in understanding. Of course—how could they have known I received their letter? They'd had no idea I was coming to Dubno.

Aaron said that he'd gone to the head NKVD official and retrieved my belongings. They divided the belongings amongst themselves. Among the pile of keepsakes and heirlooms, they came across a leather coat. Holding the coat in her hand, Aaron's sister Helene said, "This must be left for Wolf, in case he returns."

Aaron now rummaged through a few containers to find the leather coat. He held the jacket delicately and handed it to me with both hands. I could smell my father's shop in the jacket. I stared at it in my arms, letting my fingers run along the seams, absorbing the soft skin. I couldn't believe they were gone.

My voice cracked. "And what about my mother?"

Aaron froze. A shadow passed across his face. "You need to talk to Sashik, the clergyman," Aaron said without looking at me.

I never did locate Sashik, and so I never learned about my mother while in Dubno. I departed the following day with my leather coat and headed to the Hungarian front. My visit to Dubno made me feel more like a refugee than ever before. My home was gone, my purpose and direction in life that much more uncertain.

Years later in the United States, Aaron and I met with a few other survivors and exchanged stories. Aaron had a little too much to drink and began rambling about some very painful memories. Aaron assumed that I'd met with Sashik, that I knew what happened. I did not. Aaron started talking about my mother, how remarkable her survival was, how tragic her death. I could hardly believe what I was hearing—40 years later.

Chapter 19:
Chana

My mother managed to survive into the summer of 1942—one year after I left her standing on the doorstep. "If you are hungry, don't be ashamed to ask for food," she told me. Ever the loving Jewish mother making sure that her son is cared for. But she was more than just a loving Jewish mother. She was an *eshet chayil*—a woman of valor. She gave her whole heart, her whole being to all she met—to family and stranger alike. She lived her life with valor, and met her end with the same courage.

The first week after I left began a yearlong nightmare for her. My sister was in hiding, my father and brother both killed, and my mother left alone to bear the loss. After the Ukrainians finished robbing, raping, and murdering Jews, the Germans took over and formed a *Judenrat*. Germans stole valuables and forced the Jewish population into hard labor. Hundreds of Dubno Jews were killed during the summer of 1941, and many others fell due to hunger, disease, and exposure to cold weather as months stretched into winter. My mother was one of the first to help organize a public kitchen to provide some relief to the starving and suffering population. She worked tirelessly with others to pool together whatever bits of food were available to make soup or bread. It was never enough. Hundreds of people were left without anything to eat, despite her best efforts. But it didn't stop her from trying, every day, to care for others, give every last effort, to look into their frightened eyes and assure them that she was doing everything she could for them. *Eshet chayil.*

She continued like this until April 1942. Then everything stopped.

The Germans established two ghettos. The ghetto was a horrid prison. There was scarcely enough food or water and no meaningful way to treat disease. My mother was alone, not a worker, and not a member of a worker's family. So, she was put in the second ghetto, the one with the elderly, orphaned children, and widows. She cared for children, giving them comfort, singing them lullabies. I can imagine her now. A group of frightened children, huddled around her in a cramped corner of a broken room, as she soothes them with "Oifen Pripichek," just as she sang to us as children. My mother remained confined to this ghetto with thousands of other Jews until late May 1942.

One bright morning, the Germans blared over their loudspeakers that all of the Jews in the ghetto needed to report for transport. My mother knew. She knew this would be the end. Bravely, she held onto the children, teasing them, diverting them away from the barking Nazis. Fighting tears, she looked into the children's eyes and made them feel loved—it was always important to her to make sure her family knew they were loved. And so, the somber procession of Jews, laden with whatever belongings they could carry, were loaded onto truck beds and driven to the outskirts of Dubno, where mounds of freshly dug dirt lay piled around a deep pit.

Standing on the edge of the cargo bed, with the children still clasping her legs, my mother stood tall with her head high as she surveyed the land she knew her whole life. How much had changed. The industrial and military equipment that invaded her home darkened the otherwise beautiful life she had made in Dubno. This was the place she grew up, married, and raised children. Taking a deep breath, she sighed at the senseless loss of life, the surreal catastrophe that had become her existence and that of her community. She looked at the sky, searching for answers. The afternoon sun dipped below the trees, beams slanting through branches, casting their last warm rays onto my mother's cheek.

A snarling German shepherd arched and growled, drawing my mother away from her thoughts toward the terror that lay ahead. She noticed the hate in the dog's bark as he nearly pulled away from his handlers—clearly a product of the evil of the humans that trained it. The children cried, and she pressed their faces into her sides to shield them from the snapping fangs.

Walking away from the truck, she could not help but stare at the large mounds of dirt ahead—and worry about what lay on the other side. A cloud passed over the sun, sending a breeze that rustled the leaves and gave my mother goosebumps on her arms. It was too difficult to focus on the children. She shivered, her lips turning pale.

"Clothes, shoes, jewelry," ordered a guard, pointing at three piles on the ground. Jews had been here before. As the soldiers loaded their weapons, the snap of bullets entering the chamber prompted the frightened people to begin undressing. Trembling, my mother tended to the children, crying as she crouched down to undress their little bodies, undoing little buttons, and pulling little fingers through shirts and dresses. Naked, she stood there as small groups were brought around the mounds to face the pit below.

Several hundred Jews—men, women, children—stood naked and helpless as Germans armed with machine guns sat positioned on the mounds above.[xv] My mother mouthed words of prayers, hoping that the children would not suffer. Without warning, the Germans fired a shot, instantly killing a man standing near the edge of the pit. His lifeless body crumpled over and slid down the side of the dirt. A woman screamed as she watched the blood flow from his head into the earth. The Germans laughed and indiscriminately opened fire on the Jews.

My mother's heart pounded. Bullets and bodies flew in all directions. Gunshots thundered, people screamed. There was nowhere to run. The only hope was to hide from the bullets. So, my mother dove into the pit and crawled under the corpses as the bodies of her neighbors, friends, and relatives piled above her. It was awful. Alive, my mother lay wedged in a mass grave. Blood poured over her body as the screams of the dying rang in her ears.

She remained in the pit for hours—well after the sounds of the last trucks roared away. Lying there naked with the dead pressed against her, she could only think that this was inhuman. It was incomprehensible how a person could commit such atrocities against another. Searching with her eyes through the limbs of the fallen, she spotted the glow of the moon and noticed a starry night above. Clawing her way out of the mass grave, my mother stood alone in a killing field. My mother looked at the grave in disbelief. There would be no more tears. She pursed her lips—as she was prone to do when she was determined—turned away, and fled for safety.

Exhausted and exposed, my mother couldn't go far. A few short hours would bring dawn and the risks of another day. Before daybreak, my mother came upon a small church not far outside Dubno. She quietly entered the barn in the back and hid among the livestock and hay. My mother remained hidden, naked, for several weeks, surviving on scraps of food that were tossed to the pigs. Every day was tormenting: Would she be discovered? How could she escape? Where would she go? There were no good options. So she just remained, hoping to survive the best she could.

Sashik, the clergyman, resided at the church and cared for the animals. He didn't notice my mother at first, but after several weeks, he spotted her while tending to the livestock in the barn. Sashik was surprised to see her but promised to keep her presence a secret. She shared with him the story of her survival and escape from the mass grave. Listening to her, Sashik assured her that he would do what he could to help her stay alive in the church but was unable to help her escape out of Dubno. Through June and July 1942, she remained hidden in the barn. Sashik fed the animals, provided my mother with some rags to wear, and included a little extra food in the trough for my mother to survive.

One day in August, a butcher came to the farm to collect one of the cows. There was nowhere for my mother to hide. She did her best to cover herself under the hay, but the barn wasn't particularly large. The butcher fumbled around, trying to coax the cow out of the stable. My mother was pressed in the corner with only her rags and a thin layer of hay to conceal her. The butcher swore at the cow, kicking the pile of hay. My mother let out a yelp when the butcher's boot kicked her shin, prompting the startled man to stumble backward and fall into a thick pile of steaming dung.

Enraged, the butcher roared as he flung the putrid mess from his fingers. My mother, still aching from the kick, hobbled out of the hay to ask if the man was alright. Even in such circumstances, my mother's first instinct was to care for others. *Eshet chayil.* Eyes bulging, pointing an accusatory finger at my mother, the butcher exclaimed, "*Yid!*" He stormed out of the barn shouting, "*Yid! Yid! Yid!*" as the flies trailed his feces-stained clothes.

With an injured leg, my mother couldn't go far. She limped out of the barn and entered the church, where she remained crouched in a corner, rubbing her sore leg. Sashik was away, and no one else was inside. It didn't take long for the Germans to arrive. From inside the church, my mother could hear the butcher shouting. Footsteps marched around to the barn. Searching the stable to no avail, they proceeded toward the church entrance. Before they had a chance to thrust open the doors, my mother stood, ready to confront her tormentors. No more tears; she had already survived death once. The doors swung open and the two soldiers, armed for combat, entered the church to apprehend an injured Jewish woman wearing nothing more than a few tattered rags. Both soldiers crossed their hearts as they stepped over the threshold; my mother smiled at the irony. My mother kept her head high. No trembling, no more fear. They ordered her out of the church and marched her into the center of the town.

One of the soldiers guarded my mother while the other ran off to fetch the commanding SS officer. My mother stood, impervious to the storm of hate and horror around her, fully aware that this was a situation that she would not escape. The Germans called over the loud speakers for the Jews in the ghetto to gather at the barbed wire and focus attention on the woman in the town square. They aimed to make an example out of her. While they shouted threats and warnings, my mother's thoughts turned inward. She was proud of her life. She cared for the poor. She comforted the sick. She was a devoted daughter, wife, and mother. She raised three wonderful children. She was flooded with sorrow knowing that her youngest was gone, her eldest in a stranger's home, and her middle running for his life in the midst of the cataclysm that had shattered their world.

She scanned the faces of the helpless Jews trapped in the ghetto. She closed her eyes and took a deep breath, praying for them to live their last moments free of suffering. The German warnings droned on over the loudspeaker until no space was left unoccupied along the fence line. My mother continued to ignore the barrage of threats against a group of imprisoned people, turning her focus toward the town. She stood in the marketplace where once she purchased goods for family holidays and Shabbat meals. How unbearable that this life was stolen. My mother relived those memories: the weddings, bnei mitzvahs, births, and brisses, the love, the traditions. She was gazing off peacefully, initially unaware of the SS officer's presence. It was the crack of the whip that caused her to blink and stare at the face in front of her.

She met his eyes and studied his young face. He couldn't have been much older than 20, athletic, with deep blue eyes. It was the color of his eyes that reminded her. She looked at him squarely and said, "I have a son like you, out there, somewhere." She ignored the smug look on his face. She ignored the rope tied to her legs, binding them together. She ignored the horse at the other end of the rope. In the moments before her dreadful death, my mother was thinking of me.

Those words, *I have a son like you, out there, somewhere.* Those were her last words. N'chemyeh, to whom I am forever grateful, must have made it back to Dubno after the German invasion, to relay my message: that I made it out of Dubno alive. It must have been my mother's one consolation during those final months of horror. She knew I was alive. In her soul, she knew I would survive.

The whip cracked. The horse lurched forward, pulling the rope taught, yanking my mother off her feet and flat onto the ground. The Jews stared in silence. The Germans whooped and laughed. The horse charged through the streets of Dubno, dragging my mother until she died.

I wish I'd never known what happened to my mother.

Chapter 20: Hungary

When I arrived at the Hungarian front in the fall of 1944, a sense of optimism was spreading among the soldiers: Many had the strong feeling that victory was not only possible, but imminent. It was early fall and there was a massive presence of Soviet soldiers gathering for the siege. The plan was to encircle the city. It would be early winter before Budapest was finally taken, after months of long, drawn-out battles.

One afternoon, I was busy preparing for the October offensive when an imposing man with a stern look walked up to me to ask me how things were going. Judging by his uniform, I could tell that he was a senior officer. I saluted and told him about our preparations. He stayed to chat for a few moments, asking about morale and encouraging me and the rest of my unit to keep up the fight. He patted me on the shoulder and continued on his way to interact with other soldiers. Once the official was out of earshot, several members of my unit came up to me excitedly asking what he wanted and what we discussed. I shrugged. Waving my hand, I unenthusiastically recapped the conversation. They gaped at me. "Don't you know who that was?" they asked incredulously. I frowned and scratched my head, unable to come up with an answer. They paused, looked at me, and howled. "It was Stalin!" they laughed. "No, no...that was Churchill!" they erupted. Embarrassed, I laughed along with them, waiting for someone to let me in on the joke. They continued naming every major figure from Napoleon to Trotsky. Finally, as they caught their breath, someone said, "Volodya, that was General Rodion Malinovksy." My eyebrows arched in surprise: I'd had no idea it was the revered Soviet general who took the time to meet with me. As the others continued to chuckle, I smiled—*Wolf-a-Blinder* indeed.

With the fighting set to begin at any moment, we gathered for our briefing. After the group broke up, I took my tin of soup to have my ration before the chaos started. Walking toward the embankment of the Danube, I watched the river bend, rushing around the banks with tremendous force. I began to reflect on my situation. Inspired, perhaps, by the pace of our advance, I started to see a faint glimmer of hope. Some small part of me began to slowly accept that it could be possible to live a life without my family.

With these thoughts in my mind, I heard the whistle of that damn bomb — piercing the sky. I couldn't see the bomb. I just heard the rumble of the aircraft engines, rhythmically crossing above the clouds, and that one long whistle. Eyes wide with terror, I thought to myself, *I don't want to die.* I gasped, nearly choking on my soup. Coughing and scrambling to my feet, I staggered to the nearest trench and slid like a baseball player, careening over the edge and into the pit of earth below. Artillery fire crashed from both sides of the river. Panting, I rose to check to see if I was intact from the fall. Remarkably, I hadn't broken a bone. Other than being sore, I was generally alright.

Soldiers were frantically racing past each other in the trenches. I raised a hand over my forehead to shield my eyes from falling debris as I searched the sky. "Vladimir?" shouted a familiar voice. It was the Jewish solider I'd escorted to the front. "Viktor, I'm so glad that you are alive!" I shouted back over the thundering mortars. I leaned in to apologize again for having had to escort him to the front. I was speaking a mile a minute, trying to explain or rationalize the orders, my feelings, the situation. Viktor smiled and raised his hand to stop me. "Orders are orders," he said. He was fully sincere. I could see it in his eyes. There was no ill will. I paused, nodded, and extended my hand. He shook my hand in return, easing my guilt.

A commander shouted orders to be passed down to the men in the trenches. Crouching, I made my way through the trench toward the field base camp. Once there was a lull in the artillery fire, I climbed out and made a dash for the camp. I arrived, out of breath, to find the Colonel busy shouting orders and writing instructions. "Vladimir," barked the Colonel. "It's about time you arrived," he said with a wink. He handed me a folded paper. "These are for the commanding officers on the north side of the city," he said. I rushed out with the papers, maneuvering around the debris of scattered earth, crumbled buildings, and fallen bodies.

I continued relaying messages, working on mine removal, and engaging in firefights until early 1945. By then, the Soviets had encircled Budapest. It was just a matter of time before the city would fall. We all hoped Berlin would soon follow. The Germans were torn—some abandoned their posts, others fought to the death. These last months of 1944 were incredibly dangerous. Ironically, just when I was starting to be more optimistic about—and committed to—survival, I became more aware of how close to death I came with each mission. Many times I'd been buzzed by bullets or found myself just meters away from mortar shells as they crashed to Earth—one or two steps from certain death. But until this point, it was as if I'd somehow walked through the war with an invisible protective shield. Now, in Budapest, I was constantly operating in the crosshairs.

By the end of December 1944, Budapest was encircled; the Germans were trapped, which made them even more desperate. In one of their final acts before losing the city, the Germans bombed the bridges. Initial efforts to negotiate a peaceful surrender ended in failure when the Germans killed Soviet messengers.[xvi] This enraged the Soviet commanders and further fueled resentment within the Soviet ranks. Following weeks of battle to mop up the remaining resistance, the Soviets ordered the captured Germans into forced labor. In my final field assignment, I was ordered to help with the detention and deportation of these Germans to the Soviet Union where they would be used as forced labor to rebuild what they'd destroyed. I watched tens of thousands of Germans loaded and shipped off. Having learned about their war crimes, I was proud to watch justice be served.

When I finally completed my responsibilities, I had a chance to look at the remnants of the devastation and reflect on what was happening. Fires burned on both sides of the river, wafting thick smoke into the air, obstructing the view from either end of the bridges. A few of the bridges were still passable, making the narrow paths severely overcrowded. I gathered my belongings and newfound optimism and made my way across one of the bridges. There were thousands of people crossing in both directions—some moving with a purpose, others just surveying the environment. Medics tended to injured soldiers. Engineers inspected the bridge to determine if tanks and other heavy cargo could pass. Old friends reunited. Halfway across the bridge, I noticed a familiar figure. I could only faintly make out the frame of the person, but the gait was unmistakable. Hope rose within me as I approached him. Once we were close enough to see one another, broad grins spread across both of our faces. Jake and I hadn't seen one another since we were digging trenches in Grozny. Elated, we embraced.

Budapest was littered with items the Germans lost or the Hungarians left behind. We managed to find some wine, extra rations of food, and an abandoned building with an intact fireplace. Using broken furniture for firewood, we heated the room—finally feeling some warmth. Jake and I drank and talked well into the evening, stoking the fireplace until it crackled. Jake was truly lucky to have survived. He shared stories of numerous times when bullets killed soldiers on either side of him, narrowly missing his head or back or vital organs. He'd resigned himself to thinking that he wouldn't survive, but no matter how hopeless or dire the situation, somehow he'd managed to come out alright.

Jake was surprised to learn that I had gone to Dubno. He wept along with me when I shared with him the news I learned from our home. He was relieved to know that at least some of his relatives had survived—and grateful that I'd taken the risk to go to Dubno. We toasted repeatedly to fallen family and friends, sharing stories about those we'd lost. Throwing another piece of wood on the fire, I tipped the bottle to find that we had finished the wine. We decided to spend the night by the fire and report to our respective bases in the morning. We agreed that if we survived the war, we would go back to Dubno and figure out life from there. I was drunk. Just as I was about to pull my coat over me and turn over to sleep, I called out to Jake and told him, "We are going to survive."

PART 3 – SURVIVOR

Chapter 21:
Moscow

Wandering the streets of Budapest, it was clear that the war was nearing its end, but pockets of resistance persisted. I thought about all of the places we liberated. Nazis, Soviets, and the local population had destroyed so much of these towns that they were hardly recognizable. Worse, despite being liberated, cities were not safe. Crossing through the center of Budapest, I saw starved corpses strewn about city corners. Random gunshots rang out periodically—a resistance group, a thief, or a stupid, drunk solider. I finished my last assignment in Budapest and returned to the base camp. I held the wooden spoon in my hand, recalling the kindness the old couple showed me in Rostov, and thought about what I should do with my life.

While I was away on my last assignment, Jake left a letter for me prior to his departure explaining that he had reached the age of military discharge and planned to return to Dubno. Jake's letter gave me hope that I too would soon be discharged from the army and free to figure out my next step. Unfortunately, my military internment did not end so simply.

After the Red Army liberated Budapest, some of the Russian force at the front was reassigned. My successful service was recognized by Russian commanders, who recommended me for admission to Russia's military training school in Moscow. No issue was made of my Jewish identity, and given the uncertainty of a post-WWII world, at least I had a place to go and something to do. My orders to depart for Moscow came so quickly that I never had the opportunity to inform Jake of my whereabouts or destination. At least I had the comfort of knowing he was still alive.

I departed on a crisp, early-spring morning for Moscow. I slept heavily on the train, my body demanding recovery from the endless fight. When I arrived at Moscow, the outskirts of the city were ringed with rows of trenches, barbed wire, and debris. My thoughts immediately drifted to Grozny and the misery of digging trenches for months on end. Shaking this memory away, my eyes took in the scale of the city, the Kremlin, and the broad open squares and boulevards. Despite the damage, Moscow's grandeur was impressive to behold. My sightseeing was fleeting as we were promptly corralled to the military academy to begin our training.

Moscow provided the opportunity to remain out of harm's way, but the military academy did little to ease the suffering of a bitter winter. While the war raged into its final months, I was schooled in military tactics, leadership, and logistics. The hours outside of instruction were spent in the cold tundra seeking displaced mines and discharging them. The living quarters left much to be desired, as most soldiers lived in bunker-like billets. The promise of a prestigious military career quickly faded as I endured these austere living conditions and internally questioned my identity. I reflected upon the loss of my family and struggled to envision life without them. Three months in the academy passed, and I earned officer credentials. As soon as the orders were written, many of the new officers were sent back to the front and continued to serve. It seemed liked the war would continue to drag on, and I would remain captive to it.

If the living conditions and circumstances were not bad enough, I had to deal with the Ukrainians. "*Samostinik!*" the Russian soldiers would taunt the Ukrainians. *Samostinik* was a derogatory term used by the Russians to label Ukrainians that sought German support to establish an independent Ukrainian state. With the Germans expelled from the Soviet Republic of Ukraine, these Ukrainians faced a choice: Disavow their nationalistic ideals and pledge allegiance to the Soviet Union, or face imprisonment or death. It wasn't much of a choice. The Ukrainians pledged loyalty and were conscripted into the Soviet Army. They were constantly derided by the Russians. I wouldn't have cared—except that these Ukrainians felt compelled to take out their frustrations on someone and it couldn't be the Russians. So, who else?

Jewish soldiers routinely endured anti-Semitism from Ukrainians. By then I knew something about what the Ukrainians did in Dubno, and after the war, I learned much more about how they curried favor with the Germans, serving as their henchmen in perpetrating some of the war's most horrific atrocities against Jews. In their disgraced, second-class status within the Red Army, the Ukrainians would praise the Germans for killing Jews—spewing the same Nazi propaganda that brainwashed Europe. Of course, there were also Ukrainians who rejected Nazi ideology, fought against the Germans, and even risked their lives to hide Jews from persecution. However, in the Soviet Army, these voices were mute or non-existent.

The problem was that the Ukrainians heavily outnumbered the Jews in the army ranks. Of course, the Russians outnumbered the Ukrainians, but I can't remember one time when the Russians actually came to the defense of Jews. I often argued with Ukrainians— and fistfights were a weekly occurrence. The tension within the ranks caught the attention of superiors. Colonel Fintiskov, a highly decorated officer, was informed of the infighting and issued a decree to halt such provocations. While well-intentioned, this order never fully quelled the enmity among the soldiers. Even though I was now an officer in the army, I felt like an inmate in a prison, constantly on the lookout for the next assault.

I was miserable. My entire life had been turned upside down. I had been conscripted into the Red Army. While fleeing for my life from the German invasion, I'd had no other viable option to survive and defend myself. Now, I was trapped in the Soviet Union, forced to endure living outside a Jewish community, alone in the Soviet military surrounded by Ukrainians who constantly harassed me and regularly blamed Jews for the war. I could not bear this prison sentence and was consumed with plotting a way to be released from the school, from Moscow, from the Soviet Union.

And then it happened. May 9, 1945. The war ended. Jubilation filled the corridors, streets, and villages. Celebrating with my fellow officers, we each shared our goals for life after war. Many planned to settle down and start a family. Others hoped to work for the state and rebuild what the Germans had destroyed. We learned that Stalin was planning a victory parade to celebrate the end of the Great Patriotic War. Tens of thousands of soldiers would take part, including our unit. The parade was to take place in June 1945. I convinced myself that I needed to endure Moscow for one more month. I was overjoyed—surely they would not have any need for a Polish Jew; I would be permitted to leave soon! I couldn't have been more wrong.

In the middle of our revelry, a colonel marched into the barracks and called all of the new officers to attention. We were laughing and joking—fairly tipsy from numerous toasts. But the colonel was not smiling. The smattering of laughter petered out as the colonel stood stiffly before the class, clearly demanding silence. He then raised his rifle and proclaimed that the war against the Germans was over! Officers erupted in celebration, thinking that the colonel had come to share the good news and celebrate with us. Instead, as the officers cheered, the colonel slammed the butt of his rifle down so hard on the table that he splintered the edge of the table top. He was incensed. Now confused, we ceased our celebration. The colonel said that the broader conflict was not over, that the Soviet Union must now gird itself for the long fight against capitalism.

As the colonel spoke, I thought to myself in Yiddish, *Finste de oyden* (a shroud of black covered my eyes). I could not believe that I would have to spend two more years in the Soviet military before my service obligation was complete—two more years of hell. The colonel continued to draw on the euphoria of the end of the war to motivate the officers. Whether it was the vodka or the persuasiveness of the colonel, men who moments before were dreaming of a life after war began to pledge themselves to the long fight—spitting curses on the evils of capitalistic society.

I felt as if I was drowning. In the weeks following the end of the war, the radio regularly broadcast anti-British, anti-West propaganda messages. I was utterly demoralized. Speaking out against communism or Stalin would land me in Siberia or worse. I was determined to get as far away from the Soviet Union as possible, but I had no idea how to make this fantasy a reality.

Chapter 22:
A Way Out

I became increasingly depressed about the prospect of serving two more years in the Soviet military. I had no way of knowing what awful assignment awaited me. Worse, I knew I couldn't complain. Then, a miracle happened.

One day while walking through the streets of Moscow, passing by the typical billboard postings and propaganda kiosks, I noticed a sign bearing a message that I could hardly believe was true: *Any person who was a Polish citizen prior to 1939 was permitted to leave the Soviet Union and return to Poland.* This was my chance! But how? Was this even true? I immediately went to the Polish embassy to inquire about the billboard.

I stood in front of the embassy for a long while. I was nervous about the consequences of walking in. What if there was a Soviet official inside the embassy? Would I be reported to the military command? If the army found out, would they punish me? I weighed this choice soberly. Ultimately, I concluded that if I wanted a way out, this was my best chance. Could there be negative consequences? Of course. Then again, there was no assurance that remaining in the army would leave me better off. Each day was a confrontation with the Ukrainians. And any day I could be assigned to a new command in some wretched location. I took a deep breath, looked around to make sure no one was staring at me, and walked up to the door.

Inside the embassy, I let my eyes adjust to the darkness. Looking around, I saw signs posted in Russian and Polish. It felt comforting to see the Polish signs, making me feel as though I had made the right decision. I just stood there, looking around, lost.

A pleasant girl working behind the counter called out, "May I help you?"

I felt awkward because I could hardly find the words to speak in Polish. I had not spoken the language in years. I removed my hat, smiled awkwardly at the girl, walked up to the counter, and leaned in. "I am a Polish citizen," I whispered. "I lived in Dubno until 1941, when I fled for my life after the Germans invaded. I was conscripted into the Red Army and am now in officer's school in Moscow. I noticed a sign that said citizens of Poland can return, so I am here to find out how." I was amazed that I managed to stumble through the words to explain myself, and I was still very nervous about the implications of seeking release from the Soviet Union.

The girl smiled, trying to ease my tension. "My name is Anna, and yes," she confirmed, "the advertisement you read is part of a co-operative agreement reached between the Soviet Union and Poland." She tapped her nails on the counter. "The only issue is that you are not a civilian refugee," she said. "You are a soldier. We have only helped civilians until now."

I frowned, visibly deflated. "But don't worry," Anna immediately reassured me, "I'm sure you won't be the only Polish citizen in the army looking to return home." Anna smiled, trying to allay my concerns.

Given that I was an officer at the time, requesting early military discharge and permission to leave the Soviet Union presented unique problems. It was far from clear how the military would respond to such a request: a prison sentence in Siberia, execution, or a host of other punishments were possible.

"We can help you return home, but you must follow my instructions precisely," Anna said. Sensing my increasing hesitation, she mustered a confident air. "You will need to prove that you were a Polish citizen prior to 1939, and then..." Anna exhaled, recognizing the difficulty of the last point. "You will need the permission of the Soviet military command to release you prematurely from your service."

I slumped. "How can I prove I was a citizen of Poland?" I asked incredulously. "Any record would be at least six years old and likely destroyed after years of war."

Anna looked at me sympathetically. I wasn't sure where her optimism came from, but she forged ahead. "We won't know unless we try, correct?" she answered. "Let me take care of your Polish citizenship, and you find a way to receive permission from the military."

These were two significant hurdles. How in the world would I ever be able to prove that I was a Polish citizen? I couldn't even begin to focus on the authorization from the military. I shrugged; I didn't have any other options.

"Well, Anna, what do I do?"

Anna smiled again and handed me a sheet of paper and pen. "Write a letter to the Dubno city hall," she instructed. "Explain your situation. Maybe someone will respond."

If she wasn't so sincere, I would have laughed aloud. I accepted the paper and pen. At that very moment, I recalled my first letter to Dubno from Krasnodar. Amazingly, I received a response that time. Maybe, just maybe, I would receive another. It was a long shot, but optimism began to grow within me too.

I sat at a small table to draft the letter. I suddenly realized I needed to report back for duty, so I didn't have much time to get into details. I explained who I was, my family background, and my current circumstances. I then asked for help to provide any documentation possible about my citizenship. I folded the letter and handed it to Anna.

Anna reviewed the letter, nodding as she read. "Vladimir, this is perfect," she said. "We'll send it off right away. Come back in two weeks to see if there is any news."

I looked at the letter in Anna's hands and then back at her; she was smiling confidently. It was clear she was a caring person, and I was lucky my case landed in her hands rather than those of some indifferent bureaucrat. I smiled back at Anna, thanked her, put on my hat, and walked out. I knew I'd be late getting back and would likely be punished for it—but I didn't care. I finally had a chance—however small—of getting out of this place. All I could do was wait.

Those two weeks passed painfully slowly. Each day I worried that I would be ordered to deploy to some remote outpost and never be able to pursue my request to transfer out of the Soviet Union. Each day I had to deal with the Ukrainians and the never-ending insults and fights. When the time came to return to the embassy, I couldn't tell anyone where I was going. So, I snuck away without permission, hoping to return without anyone realizing I'd been gone.

I raced to the embassy, hoping to hear some news. Standing outside the entranceway, I tried to collect myself. Still panting, I walked through the door and looked for Anna. She was busy assisting another patron. A gruff old consular officer barked, "What do you need?" Once again, I was grateful to have met Anna.

"I'm following up on a request I made with Anna," I replied. Anna looked up. Once she noticed me, she smiled, excused herself from the patron, and whispered something to her colleague, who grunted and went back to his newspaper. Anna walked out from behind her desk and into the lobby. She was much taller than I expected, standing nearly eye level with me.

Anna forced a smile. "I'm sorry, Vladimir, we don't have any news yet," she said. "We sent the message but do not know if anyone received it. Don't be discouraged. There is a lot of confusion and destruction. Try again in two weeks." Anna gave me a friendly pat on the shoulder, trying to keep my spirits up. She turned and walked back to her desk, where the annoyed patron waited.

Two more weeks. Who knew what would happen in that time frame? I sulked back to the base. To make matters worse, one of the Ukrainian soldiers had reported me missing. As soon as I returned, I was sent to a solitary confinement for 24 hours. The commanders assumed that I'd gone into town for a girl, which wasn't an uncommon occurrence at the time. Still, I'd violated protocol and sat in the box.

The next two weeks passed even more slowly than the previous two. I was growing increasingly depressed, but I needed to hide my emotions from the other soldiers. When the two weeks had elapsed, I snuck away, as before—fully expecting to be punished again. A month had now passed since I'd sent the letter. I tried to keep my expectations in check. On my way to the embassy, I told myself to prepare for no news. I nearly convinced myself that this entire effort was futile.

I entered the embassy and looked for Anna. The bitter consular officer stared at me from over his paper. This time, he didn't even acknowledge me; he just returned to his paper and resumed reading. I took a seat in the lobby and waited. After nearly an hour had passed, I stood and prepared to leave. It was at that moment that Anna breezed into the lobby. "Vladimir!" she exclaimed. "I'm so glad you came today!" She walked briskly over to me, removing her jacket as she spoke. "I was out for a meeting," she apologized. "I hope you weren't waiting long."

Anna's enthusiasm filled the room and left me nearly speechless, so I simply mumbled, "Not long at all."

"Good, have a seat here—I'll be right back," she said, pointing to the table where I'd drafted the letter a month ago.

I was both excited and nervous. Anna wasn't gone long, but the tension within me was building. The embassy was quiet that day, just a few people in the lobby filling out paperwork. A moment later, Anna popped through the door with an envelope in her hand and a broad smile on her face—as usual. "I have good news," she said happily. Sitting across from me, she handed me the envelope. "Go ahead. Open it."

I took the envelope in my hand and started to unfold the papers inside. It took a few moments for my eyes to adjust to what I was seeing, but I immediately noticed my name jump off the pages. As it turned out, Stanislaw, the same official who forwarded my letter from Krasnodar to Aaron, received this letter as well. While I was in Moscow, Jake had returned to Dubno and was making plans for life after the war. Upon receiving my letter, Stanislaw had approached Jake and shared it with him. This was the first Jake had heard of my predicament. Jake worked with Stanislaw to search city records for identification documents that proved my Polish citizenship prior to 1939. Jake drafted three copies of the documents and enclosed the originals with his response to my letter.

I could hardly believe what I was reading. I reread Jake's letter and reviewed the documents. I was stunned. I looked up at Anna, who was sitting across from me, nearly giddy. "You see, now you have the proof!" she exclaimed.

This was an amazing stroke of luck, but the reality of the next hurdle washed over us both: Convincing the Soviet military to grant me an early release would not be easy. I had no idea how I should approach the army. Anna could tell that I was at a loss. She straightened her back. "Vladimir, take these documents," she instructed, just as confidently as she spoke when I first met her. "I have made copies, which I will keep here at the embassy. Write a letter to your superior officer informing him of your situation. Make it clear that you have met with our embassy and that we support your request to return to Poland."

Anna stood. I looked at her with deep sincerity and raised the papers in display. "Thank you so very much Anna," I said. "It was not possible without you."

Smiling, Anna surprised me with a hug. "Good luck to you, Vladimir," she said. "Please let me know if there is anything else I can do to help." Her kindness and compassion had helped motivate me this far. I hoped that it would carry me on to the next step.

As I made my way back to the base, I felt like I had a new lease on life. I didn't even care if I was punished, which I was, again. As soon as I emerged from my confinement, I drafted a letter to my supervising colonel. Here I was again, tapping my pen on the paper, just as in Krasnodar, contemplating the consequences of my actions. This time, I knew that my family had been murdered. I reasoned that if I admitted this knowledge, the army would not release me. However, if I said I had reason to believe my family was alive, the army might show some compassion. The last time I wrote a letter, I'd faced uncertainty: Would I receive a response? Would I get answers regarding the fate of my family? Would I want to know the answers? This time, I felt uncertainty again: Would the army support my request or punish me for it? Who knew what was the right thing to do?

So, I began to write: *I am Vladimir Nusseyonovich. I was born in Dubno, Poland, before 1939 and was a Polish citizen. I believe that my parents are alive somewhere in Poland. I request permission to go to Poland to search for my parents. I respectfully ask that you not deny this request.*

I sat back and looked at the pithy letter and my proof of Polish citizenship. Holding the papers from Dubno, I couldn't help but smile. *Thank you, Jake,* I thought. Letting the ink dry, I thought about the choice to make this request. Here I'd made it through hell, but I was more nervous to send a letter than I was to fight in a war. What would be the point of surviving if I didn't have a chance to make a life for myself? What if the Soviets changed their minds and denied Polish citizens the opportunity to leave in the future? Consequences be damned, I wasn't going to remain helplessly captive for years in the Soviet Union. This was my only chance to get out. I attached the supporting documentation and folded the papers, ensuring there was a crisp edge on each of the flaps—marking my determination. I walked buoyantly to the post office, sent the letter, and hoped for the best. That confidence began to dissipate almost as soon as I deposited the letter.

I hadn't expected an immediate response, but when weeks went by with no word, I grew anxious. Desperate, I went to the Polish Embassy, which was now increasingly busy processing requests for Polish citizens stranded in the Soviet Union. I worked my way through a crowd of people, hoping to catch Anna's attention. Anna, still gracious, was clearly exhausted and stressed by the amount of work ahead of her. Exasperated, she rose from one of her meetings, ready to head back into her office. She looked over toward the entrance and spotted me standing there in line. Anna smoothed her hair, puffed her lips, and smiled. She walked over to me and pulled me aside. "Vladimir! What brings you here today?"

I returned her smile and pulled her aside to speak with her privately. "I wrote the letter, as you suggested, but it has been six weeks, and I have not heard a word," I said.

"Just wait a little longer," Anna counseled. "We don't want to push the military. We are planning on sending notification to all government and military officials that are responsible for Polish citizens regarding the right of those citizens to return."

I understood. I nodded appreciatively. "Alright, Anna," I said. "I see you are very busy. Thank you again." I started to turn when Anna for the second time gave me a hug. "I'll look out for you from here," she said. "Good luck, Vladimir." She turned and left to face the chaos in front of her.

I disappeared into the mass of people plowing in. I would never see Anna again, but I remained eternally grateful for her kindness and support. Poles were often vicious to Jews. Yet it was Stanislaw and Anna who were instrumental in helping me. I never forgot that.

Predictably, as soon as I returned to the base, I was sent to confinement. The other officers joked, "I hope she was worth it!" I had to admit it was funny, and I laughed right along with them. That evening, there was a news broadcast over the public address system. It began with the usual anti-Western propaganda, but then included a story that I will never forget. The announcer reported that there was a Jewish resistance mounting in Palestine against the British in assertion of the Jewish right to self-determination. I could not believe my ears: a Jewish resistance group fighting for a Jewish homeland! Tears streamed down my face as I thought, *What am I doing here? I should be there.* Suddenly, I knew exactly what I would do with my life. I would join my fellow Jews and support the establishment of a state in our ancestral homeland.

Nearly a week after the radio address, I was awakened in the middle of the night. Several officers commanded me to get dressed. They didn't explain why or where I was going or who had summoned me. Frightening thoughts raced through my mind: Would I be sent to Siberia? Imprisoned? Shot? As I was escorted to the makeshift midnight meeting room, I tried to keep my composure. I sat at a small table across from my commanding colonel. In the dim light, holding several sheets of paper, he eyed me and asked, "Did you write this?"

I trembled but breathed deeply to steady my nerves. I was well aware that this could be a dangerous situation because anything could be written on that paper. "I cannot say for certain, would you please allow me to see the document?" I respectfully replied. The colonel eyed me again and slowly slid the papers across the table. Reviewing the documents, I recognized my handwriting and the original letter I'd sent the colonel asking for my release.

I knew that my family had been murdered and knew that I had lied in the letter. I forced myself to hide a smile, inwardly grateful that at least I had a chance to leave. I nodded gravely. "Yes, sir, I believe that my parents are alive somewhere in Poland, and I want to search for them," I said.

The colonel looked at me disbelievingly. "Vladimir, we are aware of the disagreements between Ukrainian and Jewish soldiers," he said. "You of course see that we treat everyone equally under our communist system. Of course, we have also invested many resources in you, and simply letting you leave...to look for your parents...is not the primary concern of the Soviet state."

I felt faint. *They are not going to let me leave*, I thought. The colonel rapped his fingers on the table and exchanged looks with the other officer in the room. I tried to keep my composure. I nearly burst out into a rambling stream of pleas, begging them to let me go. But I knew better. I held my tongue, desperately fighting the urge to talk.

"We were going to send you to Poland!" the colonel blurted, slapping his hand flat on the table. "You speak Polish. You are familiar with the area. You *were* a loyal Soviet soldier." I ignored the insult; I was not a Russian national and had suffered plenty fighting for the Soviets.

"But with this"—the colonel waved the letter—"you leave us no choice." Suddenly, a hope rose within me. The colonel sighed. "You are not old enough to receive military discharge," he said. "You will be released from the Soviet military and are required to report to the Polish military to conclude your military service."

I nearly jumped out of my chair with delight. The colonel droned on more about the idealistic fight against the West and the need for solidarity in the Soviet sphere. I tuned out his soliloquy and tried to contain my joy and relief. I was not going to be sent to Siberia, not shot, not punished—but released!

I thanked the colonel for his compassion and echoed his statement about comradery. The truth was I couldn't wait to get out of that prison a second longer. Naturally, bureaucracy being what it is, I waited another two weeks before my release papers were processed. I received a couple hundred rubles pocket money, along with orders to report to the Polish military within three weeks. When I delivered the news of my impending departure to my superiors, they curtly stamped my papers checking me out but forced me out of my sleeping quarters; I suppose they'd noticed my happiness with the orders and wanted to punish me for it. During my last night on the Soviet base, I was ordered to spend the night in a Moscow cell with German prisoners of war.

The following morning, I awoke a free man. As long as I had a way out, I would never report to the Polish military. While in military school, I'd learned that my old friend Groinim, with whom I'd fled several years ago, was recovering in a Moscow military hospital. I didn't have much time, and I didn't want to remain in the Soviet Union any longer than necessary. Still, I couldn't leave Moscow without visiting one of my old friends who'd somehow managed to survive. I bought a bottle of vodka and went to the hospital.

I found Groinim finishing a rehabilitation treatment in a hallway—frustrated with the slow pace of recovery. The astonishment on his face when he saw me was priceless. He started to cry, explaining how glad he was that I had survived. He immediately recalled all of the horror and sorrow over our lost friends and all of the death and suffering he had witnessed. I put a consoling arm around him and smiled as I presented the vodka. He laughed and wiped away the tears. We toasted and drank for hours until we were both completely drunk. Groinim said that he was injured in Crimea—the same place I'd been heading when the train was bombed. I shared my story with him and the news of the civilian massacres. He said he'd heard similar stories but could not believe they were true. We drank and talked until we both passed out in his hospital room. I woke the next morning slumped in the chair in his room. I splashed some water on my face to wash away the hangover. I wished Groinim well and briskly walked to the train station. I left Moscow, grateful to be on my way out of the Soviet Union.

Chapter 23:
Dubno for the Last Time

I arrived in Dubno in the late afternoon. Stepping off the train, I was elated to be out of Moscow but overwhelmed with sadness and uncertainty looking around at the city I once knew. Buildings and roads were in shambles, and a gray fog seemed to linger, obscuring what would otherwise have been a nice summer day. The bustle of the marketplace was gone. The soccer fields had been destroyed by tank tracks and mortars. Walking from the station, the fencing and wires that marked the Dubno Ghetto stood as an ominous reminder of the murders. Even though I'd been in Dubno a year before and learned about the evil committed by the Ukrainians and Germans, it was difficult to reconcile the town of my childhood with the place I saw before me. It quickly became obvious that Dubno was no longer my home and would never be again.

I spent several days in Dubno, finding out whatever I could about relatives and friends—everyone weathered, older, a part of their souls stolen. Of the approximately 300 Dubno Jews who survived the war, only a few dozen remained in the city—and they were lost: Some wandered, others continued in their regular routines, some planned on leaving Europe for more welcoming lands.

Even with the war over, Dubno was not particularly safe for Jews. Ukrainians were stealing from the homes and shops of deceased Jews with no heirs to claim them. Amidst the sorrow, there was some quiet talk of revenge. It was fairly well known that the city's Ukrainian population had blood on their hands. Some were brazen, proudly claiming to have killed hundreds of Jews. A handful of the Dubno Jews plotted to kill some of the Ukrainians for their crimes, but as far as I know none ever did. What was the point? Killing the Ukrainians would be justified revenge, but would almost certainly cause one of us to be killed or imprisoned in retaliation. Rebuilding in a land teeming with anti-Semites was futile. The best option was to leave Europe for good.

Jake was in Dubno, resuming his trade of shoemaking while exploring his options to leave Europe. While I was trying to get out of Moscow, he met Eva, a Polish Jew from a nearby town who had also miraculously managed to survive the war. He and Eva planned to marry, which seemed sudden to me—but then again, when we'd barely escaped with our lives, why wait?

I was happy for Jake. Even though he wasn't sure where he was going or what he was going to do, he seemed committed to doing it with Eva. I shared my experience in Moscow and how I'd heard about the fight to establish a Jewish homeland. I had decided in Moscow that I had no intention of reporting to the Polish army and was already planning on a future life fighting for a worthy cause: the establishment of a Jewish state. The desire to support a Jewish homeland was strong, but from within Dubno, my thoughts swirled in confusion. Sitting near the mass graves of my family and friends, it became difficult to see a way forward.

I wallowed in despair, spending long days with Jake, tormenting myself about what more I could have done to protect my brother and sister. I couldn't stand being in Dubno, but I couldn't bear to pull myself away. I couldn't even tolerate Dubno for a full day without drinking. I numbed myself with vodka. I drank so heavily one day that I became violently ill. Jake was with me the entire time, giving me space to drown my sorrows while ensuring that I didn't do anything dangerous or stupid. The following morning, with my head splitting and insides churning, Jake brought me tea, water, and bread. He sat with me in silence as I nursed myself out of my hangover. It was obvious that I needed direction, but I was so volatile that the wrong words or tone would send me into a bitter tirade or self-destructive binge. Jake could see I was hurting, and he was always good at finding a way to make things better. He didn't comment on my drinking. He didn't criticize my feelings. He casually observed, "Eliminate the Diaspora, or the Diaspora will surely eliminate you." I smiled. Jake was right. Jabotinsky was right. I needed to get out of Europe. There was nothing left for me in Europe. There was nothing left for Jews in Europe. Jake's nudge gave me just what I needed—enough distance from the loss, from the pain, to look at my life.

I turned to Jake. "How do I get out of here?" I asked. Jake said that he'd heard about a Zionist organization operating out of Bratislava that was organizing a movement of Jews to return to their ancestral home in Palestine. Jake also told me that our cousin Manny Grossberg was alive and working in a bakery in Bratislava. It was settled: I would go to Bratislava and find my way out of Europe. Jake provided me with a suit that was in good condition—enough to pass as a civilian. I bid Jake farewell and promised to send him my location once I knew where I was going. We also had family members in the United States, so we agreed to send them our locations and plans, in the event we could not reach one another directly.

With still another week left to report to the Polish military, I took one last walk around the town. I walked to my street but could not bear to go any closer to my house. I replayed in my mind scenes from my happy, mischievous childhood. The soccer ball I made of my father's shoes. The Maccabi games. Playing second baritone in the band. Peeking through the wall at Sarah's clients. Helping my mother prepare for Jewish holidays and the Sabbath. Going to the synagogue with my father. And, again, I had a stabbing memory of waving off my brother when he begged to leave with me. Bleary-eyed, I wiped the tears from my face and turned to walk away from my home forever. I never saw Dubno again.

As I took my seat on the train, I leaned my head against the window and noticed the grief in my reflection. As the train whistled and pulled away, I watched Dubno disappear into the twilight. My mind swirled with memories, eventually settling on the last Passover we spent together. I could see it vividly: the small gathering of our immediate family around the dining room table with my father sitting next to me. I remembered the planes flying overhead, my father looking up, then at all of us. And then I remembered his words: "G-d only knows if we will be together next Passover."

He knew. He would try to save Sarah. He would try to keep his family intact. But even then he knew that the wave of hatred and violence that was rising in the West would be too much to withstand. I was too naïve then to appreciate it. How I wish I could go to him then, to show him my gratitude for all that he'd done for us, to let him know I understood how difficult and painful the situation was—to tell him how proud I was of him.

And then I thought of my brother and sister. I recalled all of the soccer games with my brother, and the many walks we would take while running errands for our mother. I loved how he looked up to me. I loved how he was so protective of Sarah. A smile creased my face as I remembered Sarah cursing me out when she learned that I used to peek at her clients through the wall. I was also her first baby brother; she used to play with me and tend to me as a child. I could feel the void within me now that they were gone.

Finally, I thought of my mother. Aaron had said there was more to the story, but I wouldn't learn the rest for many more years. I never located Sashik, the clergyman, and so I rode that train away from Dubno with more questions about my mother than answers. It was her strength and her grace that I remembered. As the train rolled into the night, memories of my mother washed over me. I recalled the Yiddish lullabies she used to sing to us as children. I closed my eyes, listening to her voice in my mind, and fell asleep.

Chapter 24:
Greeks

I arrived at Bratislava the following morning and the city was bustling with activity. There was a large military presence, but it appeared as though the reconstruction effort was already underway. I staggered off the train, sleep-deprived and unfamiliar with my surroundings. Buildings and roads were still in awful disrepair, making it difficult to navigate the streets.

It took a couple hours of searching, but finally I met someone who knew of a Jewish baker but did not know the baker's name. He escorted me to the street where the bakery was located. It was Manny's. The smell of the knishes wafted in the air, drawing me closer to the location. Standing outside the small shop, I could not help but smile with pride—at least another one of my relatives had survived.

I walked in, fully aware of my attire, and proclaimed in Russian that I was there to conduct an inspection of the owner's license and papers. I heard the pots crash in the kitchen, followed by a thunder of Yiddish curses. It took all my self-control not to burst out laughing. Suddenly, a tall man wearing an apron came out and stammered in Russian about his business. As he approached me, his eyes moved away from my uniform and toward my face. Locking eyes, he stopped. I could not hold it any longer; I howled with laughter, and Manny's face erupted in a broad grin. He wagged a finger at me and cursed at me further for giving him a fright. He then began to laugh, and we embraced one another with tears of joy streaming down our cheeks.

Manny and I spent the rest of the afternoon and evening exchanging survival stories. Manny explained that Bratislava was still under Soviet occupation but close enough to the British occupation zone to allow refugee assistance and underground Jewish movements to operate. Manny was also planning to leave Europe and arranged for me to meet with a man by the name of Avrum, the chief organizer of the underground movement in Bratislava. Sensitive to the urgency of my situation—I was, after all, deserting the Polish Army—Avrum agreed to meet me that night.

Avrum explained that his job was to help Jewish survivors relocate to displaced persons camps in Italy, Germany, and Austria. Avrum kept looking at my hands and asked if he could see my wrists. I didn't understand why but turned them over anyway. Avrum exhaled a sigh of relief, but his face still seemed puzzled. "Partisan?" he asked. I told him that I fled Dubno as a refugee at the start of the war and then was conscripted in the Red Army. Avrum nodded. "We have met a few people like you, but not many," he said. "Most were not fortunate enough to escape so early, and only a few that did managed to survive."

Perplexed about the wrist, I asked why he looked. Avrum hesitated. "You don't know, do you?"

"Know what?" I asked, confused and worried.

Avrum then explained the horrific process of the concentration camps, the gas chambers, the ovens, the falling ashes—and the tattoos. I looked at my wrists and thought of the Romanians. How much worse could this get? I told Avrum that I'd heard stories in Romania about massacres, mass graves, death marches. My anger boiled over. How in the hell had the world allowed this to happen? Someone must have known that these train cars crammed with people were sent to extermination camps. I raged and cursed while Avrum patiently listened; he'd had this conversation before.

I wanted revenge, blood. I asked Avrum how we could make the Germans and their accomplices pay for this. Avrum was calm. He said that Germany was defeated. There was nothing else we could do to punish them for their evil and for their crimes. However, there was something we could do to ensure that Hitler's plans would ultimately fail. I looked up, intrigued. He simply said, "Survive." I exhaled, unsatisfied. "Listen, Wolf, survive this war," Avrum urged. "Start a new life. Have children. Pass our traditions to future generations. This is the only way to ensure that the Nazis will have failed."

Through my anger, I could see that Avrum was right. Who would I kill? The Germans were destroyed. My family was gone. There was only the future. Holding my Soviet military hat in my hand, I realized that I didn't really have many options and going back to Poland to serve in the Polish Army was certainly not one of them. I unclenched my fists and took a deep breath. "Nu, Avrum, what shall I do?"

Avrum smiled and poured us each a shot of vodka. I held up the glass, forced a smile, and toasted, "L'chaim." Avrum looked over at me sincerely. "Yes, and to the future," he added. Feeling the familiar burn of the drink slide into my stomach, I was ready to listen. Avrum worked with the American Jewish Joint Distribution Committee (JOINT/JDC), which, with the assistance of a variety of other organizations, could help provide me with money, transportation to a displaced persons camp, and support to relocate to another country. Avrum explained that Bratislava was the heart of Jewish emigration out of Eastern Europe, often assisting displaced Jews that had lost their homes and businesses to find a new life in Palestine. When the Germans arrived in September 1944, the city's approximately 2,000 remaining Jews were sent to Auschwitz. In April 1945, after the liberation of the city, the Jewish community was reestablished, just a few months before my arrival. Avrum said there were plans to revive the Jewish community. Later that year, Bratislava would hold High Holiday prayer services in the synagogue. Schools, kosher butchers, and other community services were to follow eventually.[xvii] Avrum's speech was all very impressive, and the rapid resurgence of a Jewish community in Bratislava somehow made me feel optimistic about the future. Still, I wanted no part of Europe: *Eliminate the Diaspora, or the Diaspora will surely eliminate you.*

Avrum said the first thing I needed to do was discard my Soviet uniform. My only other clothes were my leather jacket and the suit that Jake had provided me. Avrum said he would arrange for me to have false documents stating that I was a concentration camp survivor. He sensed that I was uncomfortable representing myself as a camp survivor but explained that it was necessary to avoid any potential scrutiny in the future. He informed me that there was a secret meeting scheduled for the following evening to prepare the next group of survivors for escape to a displaced persons camp.

The following evening, Avrum and a group of approximately 50 Jews from a variety of Eastern European and Soviet Republic backgrounds met in an abandoned flat. The following day, Avrum explained, we would walk across the Soviet border into British-occupied territory. Asked how we would do this, Avrum answered that the border was poorly manned and that should anyone question us, we would claim to be Greeks who'd been held in concentration camps and were making our way back home. Some protested that no one spoke Greek. "Neither do the guards," Avrum replied. The plan was to meet in small groups inside the city and make our way to a landmark outside the city center where we would all join together in one large group.

With my new false papers and civilian clothing, I joined hundreds of other Jewish refugees the following morning. It was an awe-inspiring site: a group of Jews who had defied the odds of survival banding together to walk toward freedom and the opportunity for a new life. Avrum was right: Survival is the best revenge.

Despite the hollow sadness within every person's eyes, there was laughter, camaraderie, and hope. An organizer stood on a rock to address the crowd. Speaking Yiddish in a foreign accent, he explained that we would proceed together toward the British border. A small girl would lead the way, followed by a group of the most able-bodied men; behind them, all of the other survivors. The purpose of the men behind the girl was to signal a peaceful group but one that would immediately defend the safety of the girl. The organizer shouted a few Greek phrases, in case we would need to speak, but no one committed the words to memory—either we would cross peacefully, or we would fight to cross.

It took several days of walking, but we eventually reached the border. As the head of the underground had guessed, the border at our point of crossing was unmanned; we simply walked out of the Soviet Union and into the West.

We were so elated that we didn't even mind the additional few hours of walking to reach a British military base. The JOINT representatives had a contact operating there who was expecting our arrival. We were housed in tents and provided with basic food and water. People rubbed sore muscles, gratefully filled their rumbling stomachs, and spoke openly as only free people can. Gulping down some water, I noticed a few people standing at the edge of the field solemnly mumbling prayers while staring off toward a pillar of smoke. Looking toward the horizon, I noticed in the distance a burning structure. It looked like every other fire I'd observed during the war, so I couldn't quite understand why this group of Jews cared so much about it.

I left the others who were smiling and splashing their faces to inquire about the smoke on the other side of the field. As I walked toward the solemn group, one of the JOINT staff walked by. I stopped him to ask what was burning in the distance. He stopped suddenly and gave me a sympathetic look. Exhaling, he looked toward the rising smoke and said that it was a Nazi concentration camp. The gravity of those words blunted any joy I had experienced moments earlier. The young man looked back at me again, nodded politely, and left me to stand silently absorbing what he'd said. With Avrum's description of the camps still fresh in my mind, I felt an overwhelming sense of sadness and helplessness. How senseless the loss of life. All of those innocent people slaughtered in these murder factories. I crossed the field to join the solemn group. Some people only stayed a moment; others much longer.

I looked around at the fields and sky, trying to reconcile a beautiful summer evening with the billowing stain in front of me. My blood boiled as I glared at the black smoke, dissipating into the clouds. Following the lead of others, when I was overcome with grief for the pain of all those who'd suffered so cruelly, I started to recite the words of the Mourner's Kaddish.

Maybe it was because the war was over; maybe it was because I was free from the Soviet Union; maybe it was because I finally had the chance to think about something other than survival. Whatever triggered it, I cried and wailed. I convulsed, grieving for my murdered family, for the loss of my community, and for the indescribable pain I witnessed and experienced during the war. This was the only time in my life that I ever fully surrendered to my grief, leaving myself entirely vulnerable to express the torment inside me. I shouted to the stars, pleading for forgiveness—for leaving my family, for leaving my brother when he begged to join me. I implored my parents to guide me, to provide me with the strength to go on. I fell to the ground and sobbed. No one came to check on me; fits of hysteria and screams in the night were a frequent occurrence among Holocaust survivors. The tears left my eyes bleary and my body depleted. Grief poured out of me so intensely that I lost consciousness. I fell asleep in the dirt on the edge of the field.

The pain never left; it just became a part of me. The next morning, I pulled myself together and rubbed my eyes to adjust to the early light. Most people were already awake, sipping hot cups of steaming tea. Disheveled from sleeping outdoors in my clothes, I stumbled over to a group of people chewing breakfast biscuits. They invited me to join them for a cup of tea. I must have looked pathetic, judging from the pity in their eyes. Then again, they'd all been through their own hell. Speaking with them, it became clear that we survivors were a large collection of uprooted individuals. We were alone, with no one to rely upon but distant relatives and one another. There were no couples, no family members. Our immediate families had been murdered.

In the depth of our soul-searching to find new meaning in our lives, many of the single people among us found that future in one another. There were only a handful of people from any given town or village who survived. Among the few survivors from each town, incredibly strong bonds often formed—bonds of shared history, of shared memories. I guess they felt it was *besheret*—it was meant to be—that they should find each other. Even though we were all poor and lost, it was beautiful to witness so many young men and women fall in love and get married on our journey.

We spent a few short days in British-occupied Austria. There were undoubtedly others that would be pouring in from across the Soviet border and Western Europe and a temporary tent camp in Austria would not accommodate the need. We had to move on somewhere, at least for the time being. One of the JOINT organizers called us all to a meeting to explain our next steps. Since we claimed to be Greeks, the plan was to relocate us south, to a displaced persons camp in Italy, with the goal of eventually processing us to our ultimate destinations. A train operated by the British would transport us to Italy. We didn't think much about it at first, since getting way from Germany and the Soviet Union was all we cared about in the moment. But that would change once we boarded the train.

The coach cars echoed with a cacophony of Yiddish dialects, Russian and Eastern European languages, prayers of gratitude, concern over the security of the journey ahead. Initially, the mood was generally optimistic. However, the sour looks on the faces of the British soldiers made it clear they weren't too pleased with their orders. At the time, the British were fighting Zionist Jews for control of Palestine, and a few of the Jewish survivors observed that British train conductors might be unwilling to abet the flight of European Jews who might end up in Mandatory British Palestine fighting their countrymen. This set off hysteria.

Men shouted that the British couldn't be trusted. Women cried, fearing they would be transported to Germany. The tension on the train boiled over, with anger and fear spilling out of the mouths of the survivors. The British, who couldn't understand a word, loaded their weapons out of concern, prompting an escalation of fear among the Jews. The JOINT representatives tried to defuse the situation, assuring us that the British operated the trains and the journey would never stray outside of British- or American-controlled territory—but they were drowned out by the panic on the train. The JOINT representatives pleaded with us to calm down and advised the British soldiers to step away from the train to avoid an unnecessary confrontation.

The JOINT staff repeatedly assured us that the British would take us to Italy, but this failed to satisfy our group because we all assumed that the British realized that we were not Greek refugees. Vocal Jews adamantly insisted that several Jews sit together with the train conductor to ensure that the train did in fact stay on course for Italy. The bickering between the JOINT representatives and Jews continued, with an interpreter relaying bits and pieces of the discussion to the increasingly impatient British soldiers.

It was just when we seemed to have reached an intractable impasse that a senior British officer entered the scene and calmly walked to his soldiers, ordering them to draw down their weapons. He surveyed the mass of people nervously crowding around or standing inside the train car. The officer carried an unforgettable gravitas that commanded the attention of all those in his presence. He spoke with clarity and grace. He approached the JOINT representative and explained that the British were honored to volunteer to help the "Greek" refugees for humanitarian reasons. If it would make the refugees more comfortable, they were welcome to ride with the conductor. The JOINT staff translated the officer's words, which instantly assuaged the fears of the survivors. With that delicate stroke of diplomacy, the argument was resolved and the train pulled out of Austria.

The ride was uneventful. We rolled along magnificent landscapes of green hillsides and soaring mountains which bore no evidence of war. It was a strange feeling to be free of orders, of constant hunger, of war. I struggled to accept that I was alone in the world. I'd been forced by circumstances to become independent at an early age, so I was comfortable being on my own; and since I always looked for the humor in life and was outgoing, I made friends easily. Still, the ache of never seeing my family again and knowing how they must have suffered in those final hours tore at me—even if it stayed hidden just below the surface of my smile.

Chapter 25: Displaced Person

JOINT provided each of us with an index card that we would use to record our entries and exits as we bounced from one location to another. The train arrived in Rome, and I received my first entry: Cinecitta—the famed Italian movie studio. Cinecitta was divided into two camps, one for Italians and colonized Libya and Dalmatia, and another international camp.[xviii] This was the first time I'd ever seen and met people from outside of Europe. There wasn't much time to get to know them as we spent just one short week at Cinecitta before being shipped back north to Milan. After a few more weeks, I was eventually routed to Cremona, where I would remain for a couple years. Cremona, which housed approximately 1,100 refugees while I was there, was one of the largest displaced persons (DP) camps in northern Italy. In 1948, we were moved to the Barletto DP camp in Southern Italy, where I remained until September 1949.[xix]

In the summer of 1946, Cremona suffered a severe clothing and food shortage. Sorely needed aid packages destined for the camp were stolen and sold on the black market; and, of course, we were all too poor to pay black market prices. Some in the DP camps died of hunger or disease. Others simply left. We all contributed somehow to providing for one another. Everyone who knew a trade pitched in;

those who didn't learned in the vocational school. Tailors and seamstresses worked to make and mend clothes. Men cut lumber. Women peeled potatoes and prepared large vats of soup. Teachers developed lessons for children. We also held Jewish celebrations: dances, Purim shows where children dressed in costumes, and Zionist marches and gatherings to support the establishment of the State of Israel.

Health care was a constant area of need. Most of the survivors had numerous health problems and tending to these ailments with limited supplies was a challenge. I considered myself very lucky: Other than suffering from some malnutrition, my main need was dentures to replace some teeth damaged during the war.

I remember walking into the health clinic and meeting the overworked Italian dentist struggling to keep pace with the demand for his services. As I sat in the waiting room, I looked at all the people holding their jaws, each desperately needing dental care. The thought dawned on me that if I could learn the dental trade, I would have the skills to support myself and earn a decent living. Isacco, the dentist, called my name and examined my teeth.

It turned out that Isacco was an Italian Jew who managed to escape persecution by pretending to be a Christian. Since I hardly spoke more than a few phrases in Italian, and Isacco knew only a handful of specific terms in Yiddish, we had a difficult time communicating. We did a lot of speaking with our hands. He recommended that my decaying teeth be pulled and that I get fitted for dentures. I frowned but agreed to have him proceed. I then asked Isacco if he had any assistants. He said that most of the people he was able to retain helped with administrative tasks or general cleaning of his laboratory, but as far as technicians, he was on his own. I told him that if he was willing, I would work for him as an apprentice. Isacco smiled and agreed.

The next day I reported for duty. Isacco explained that I would need to go through a lot of schooling and training to be a dentist, but that I could more practically learn to be a dental technician, focusing on making dentures. Isacco was a patient teacher, showing me the fundamentals of taking impressions and preparing molds for dentures. Unfortunately, when we were transferred to Barletto, I lost contact with him. I never did see Isacco again, but I remained forever grateful to have learned the basics of a skill that would be the source of my livelihood in years to come.

When I wasn't working in the dental lab, I learned Italian, joined a soccer league, and took part in Jewish cultural events. I was grateful to be alive, of course, but I was far from happy. The war had imposed structure on my life: missions, gathering food, focus on survival. Now the war was over. I was freed from my internment in the Soviet military and had escaped the oppressive, anti-Semitic regimes that had governed my entire previous life. Life in Cremona and Barletto was like living in a holding pattern—people moving in and out, migrating on to somewhere else. It was a constant reminder that life there was only temporary. The thought in the back of my mind was always, *What will I do now?* I missed my father's guidance more than ever.

JOINT saw to our practical needs—providing shelter, food, health care, and even helping to organize a *shechita*, or ritual slaughter, of kosher beef. The organization also helped us establish contact with friends and relatives in other countries that could absorb us. There was a central location where refugees could register and seek relatives. The kind young ladies working at the registry suggested that we contact any relatives we knew of to explore as many relocation options as possible. No one knew how long it would take to leave a displaced persons camp—some people would leave within a few months, others had to wait much longer.

Shortly after my arrival at Cremona in 1945, I sought JOINT's assistance in locating good addresses for the few relatives that I had outside of Europe. I did not know of any relatives on my father's side who had survived. On my mother's side, I had three cousins in Palestine—Rosali, Dov, and Abraham—who lived on a small kibbutz. I also had an Uncle Samuel who lived in New York. Those were my only contacts in the outside world. I prepared two letters asking for their help. I explained that my entire immediate family was killed and I was the only remaining survivor. I added that Jake and I survived the war together—and that the last I knew he was still in Dubno. I sent the letters and waited. Most of that fall passed before I finally received a response.

The first response I received was from my Uncle Sam in New York. He wrote that the United States had a quota for Polish immigrants and that entering the U.S. in that capacity could take years. The other option was to come to the United States as a student. He offered to help me with my admission application if I was interested. He also mentioned that he'd heard from Jake, who was making plans to relocate to America.

Nearly a month after Sam wrote, I received a letter from my cousin Abraham. He wrote that he would do what he could to facilitate my relocation to Palestine, provided that was what I wanted to do. During the rest of my years in Italian DP camps, I grew to depend heavily on Abraham's letters. His words reminded me of my father and offered the same thoughtful questions and guidance I so missed. He promised to help and guide me in finding the best path forward.

It would take a few years for Sam to secure a visa for me, but by early 1949, I had in my hand the documents I needed to enter the United States. Throughout the intervening years, I had continued to be haunted by the memory of the news report crackling over the loudspeaker in Moscow about a Jewish resistance in Palestine. I felt guilty for even considering anything other than joining my Jewish brothers and sisters in building a Jewish state, the one silver lining to emerge from the ashes of the Holocaust. Ultimately, it was Abraham who helped reconcile me to my choice. "In every man's soul there is fight between materialism and idealism," he said. "If you choose to come to the land of Israel and live simply on a kibbutz, you will have the provisions you need and have the opportunity to live in the ancestral Jewish homeland." On the other hand, he noted, I had an uncle in the U.S. and a chance for an easier life there. It was clear that I was faced with a choice between idealism (working to establish a Jewish state) or materialism (the opportunities in the United States). After four years of war and four more years of bureaucracy, I was tired. My entire life as a young man had been consumed by war. I felt that the U.S. would provide an easier life, a life of opportunity. At 27 years old, I was tired of war and chose opportunity over idealism.

It was just before I departed Cremona that I made the choice to come to America. It would take another two years in Barletto before I received the final approval to immigrate. Even after I made my choice, I continued to wrestle with my conscience during those last two years in Barletto—and the opinions of my fellow refugees did little to resolve this conflict. For each person who passionately advocated moving to the only Jewish homeland, there was another who believed just as strongly that one should seek stability in the West. Abraham continued to write letters of encouragement, sympathizing with my dilemma. He enabled me to see that moving to America was not an abandonment of Israel, since I would always be able to connect with the land and people of Israel. Abraham's guidance was certainly what I needed at the time, but it never fully resolved the struggle within me about that choice.

It was at around the same time that I made my decision to immigrate to America that a simple act would leave a lasting impression on me—inspiring me with hope for the future. Preparing to depart Cremona for Barletto with other refugees, I heard one of the JOINT organizers call us over for a group photograph. Everyone smoothed their hair and clothes, trying to look as presentable as possible. There was a large group of us, perhaps several hundred. The photographer asked for all of the survivors to come close together. As we shuffled our feet toward one another, I looked at the men, women, and children standing around me. These were exceptional people who had endured the worst of humanity and pulled themselves together through the pain and grief to start new lives. I was suddenly overwhelmed and proud to stand among them. As I scanned the faces of these incredibly brave individuals, the words of the photographer echoed in my mind—"Survivors, come closer together." A profound feeling washed over me: I am a survivor.

Epilogue, From the Author

My father arrived in the United States in September 1949. His Uncle Sam owned a restaurant on 42nd and Broadway in New York and gave him a job and a place to stay. It was difficult grunt work, working in the bowels of the kitchen, but at least he had a roof over his head and some money in his pocket. Sadly, Uncle Sam did little else to help him acclimate and assimilate into the U.S. The choice to come to America instead of Israel began to look like a mistake. After spending a year working long, hard hours, he started to look for other opportunities.

As it turned out, other opportunities found him. The U.S. was embroiled in the Korean War, and he was drafted. My father was grateful to live in the U.S. and wanted to make a contribution, but he could hardly stomach facing combat in another war. He was concerned that if he protested the draft call, he might be sent back to Europe. So he answered the call and served in the U.S. Army at Fort Carson, Colorado, for two years. He never had to deploy overseas, and by the time he was honorably discharged, he was glad to have served the country that had welcomed him.

While at Fort Carson, he refined his skills as a dental technician, which served as the foundation for his future career. He married his first wife, Helen, and had three sons: Nate, Lee, and Seth. Nate died in a tragic accident as a small child, which ultimately led to my father and Helen's divorce. 17 years later, my father met my mother, Bronia, in Israel. At 53, he started his second family, raising me and my younger sister, Sonia. By the time my father passed away in February 2014, he had lived to meet and play with five grandchildren: Edan, Olivia, Hannah, Lev, and Eker. Two years later, my wife Rachel and I welcomed our son, Jonah, named after my father.

My father remained conflicted his entire life about the choice to emigrate to the U.S. or Israel. He was an ardent supporter of the

Jewish state and the right of Jewish self-determination. He traveled frequently to Israel and donated many trees to be planted. While never religious, he was proud of Jewish heritage, culture, and tradition. While a patriotic American, my father maintained his ties to friends and relatives in Israel—never letting go of the precious relationships that survived WWII and the Holocaust.

My father loved Colorado and the outdoors. He called it G-d's country. An avid skier, he taught us all to love the sport, which he continued to enjoy until he was 81.

My father had an incredible sense of humor—and plenty of *chutzpah* to go along with it. He could make a party of any gathering, infecting everyone with his exuberant laugh and witty jokes. He brought light and joy to the people he met, and it was this light that helped him survive the unspeakable darkness of WWII.

Author's Note to the Reader

I was seven years old, sitting in the kitchen with my younger sister and the babysitter. My parents had been out to dinner with some friends from the "old country." We heard the garage door open and were excited to tell them about our evening.

The moment the door opened, it felt as if all of the air in the room was instantly swallowed in a vacuum. All excitement dissipated, and it was as if time stopped. The ambient noise disappeared. Even at seven, I could sense something was wrong. It was one of those experiences that imprints on your memory—all my senses capturing the moment. I remember my father walking through the door with his eyes cast down, brooding, staring at the floor as he moved slowly through the kitchen and toward the bedroom. I remember his brown suit. I remember the creaks of the floorboards.

I remember my mother putting on a brave face, forcing a weak smile as she prepared to address our puzzled expressions. "Your father learned about what happened to his mother, and he is very sad," our mother explained tenderly. We knew our father had survived a war but were too young to understand the gravity of the moment.

I grew up with random stories about my father's family, but the story of his survival, his loss, his guilt, was something he rarely discussed. Ten years later, with that profound feeling from the kitchen still etched in my memory, I asked my father for his permission to document his survival story—for posterity, for our family. At 65 years old, he agreed to spend a few days answering my questions. Those were extremely difficult conversations. I was not prepared to deal with the burden he bore. He agonized over the loss—tearing at himself, blaming himself. He initially refused to discuss his mother, a topic so painful that he became physically sick just talking about it. When a topic became too emotional, he shifted immediately to pride—underscoring the accomplishment of defeating the Germans, averting the scars left by war.

These recordings remained dormant until I graduated from college. Five years after our initial conversation, I reviewed my notes and asked him to dedicate one more week to filling in the gaps. This was the last time we discussed the intimate details of his survival. The conversations were just as painful the second time, and again, I found myself struggling to contain my own emotions watching my father clench his fists and cry. He never cried.

It was never possible to learn everything that happened. Some things he couldn't recall. Others he refused to share, somehow hoping that this would erase the nightmares from his memory. When I reviewed the final outline with him and shared my plans to draft a memoir, he approved. He gave me his blessing and said he was proud of me for putting it together. The story of his survival ended with his arrival in the United States, but the story of his life would continue for nearly 70 more years.

The events in the book are true—based on interviews with my father and supplemented by research of the historical record. However, to enhance the experience for the reader, I created dialogue and narrative description that approximate what might have plausibly occurred based on my father's testimony but which are otherwise undocumented.

In my father's honor, and for all those who survived or perished in the Holocaust, I am dedicating a share of the proceeds from this memoir to the United States Holocaust Memorial Museum and Yad Vashem.

I thank you for reading my father's story and hope that you are as inspired by it as I was.

Photos

Bottom row, left to right: Wolf Vofk (Eisharik); Wolf Kogul (Blinder); Jake Grossberg; Motel Grossberg; Wolf Grossberg (Shvartze); Avrum (Loda); Zeisel Grossberg

Middle row, left to right: Vofk (Eisharik's mother); Einder (Jake's sister); three boys are nephews to Eisharik's mother; Babi Leah (Chana Kogul's mother); Moshe Kogul (Wolf's brother); Sarah Kogul (Wolf's sister); Fayge Grossberg; unknown (Manny Grossberg's sister)

Top row, left to right: Avrum; Toybe; Herzel; unknown woman; Moshe Grossberg; Chana Kogul (Wolf's mother); Sam Grossberg (uncle in New York); Kaile; Ynke Grubman; Manny Grossberg; unknown (Manny Grossberg's brother)

Leather coat provided by Aaron during last visit
to Dubno. Woman on left unkown.

Sara Kogul (left). Person on right unknown

DP camp soccer

DP camp soccer (far left)

References

i. http://www.yadvashem.org/righteous/stories/graebe/hermann-friedrich-graebe-affidavits

ii. http://www.jewishvirtuallibrary.org/dubno-jewish-history-tour

iii. https://en.wikipedia.org/wiki/Kremenets#Jews_of_Kremenets

iv. http://www.yadvashem.org/untoldstories/database/index.asp?cid=554

v. http://www.yadvashem.org/untoldstories/database/index.asp?cid=515

vi. http://www.yadvashem.org/righteous/stories/kharkov

vii. http://www.yadvashem.org/righteous/stories/kharkov

viii. http://www.yadvashem.org/untoldstories/database/index.asp?cid=283

ix. http://www.yadvashem.org/untoldstories/database/index.asp?cid=375

x. http://www.yadvashem.org/untoldstories/database/index.asp?cid=375

xi. http://www.yadvashem.org/untoldstories/database/index.asp?cid=1044

xii. http://www.yadvashem.org/odot_pdf/Microsoft%20Word%20-%205936.pdf

xiii. http://www.yadvashem.org/untoldstories/database/index.asp?cid=1044

xiv. http://www.yadvashem.org/holocaust/about/final-solution-beginning/romania

xv. http://www.yadvashem.org/yv/en/about/institute/killing_sites_catalog_details_full.asp?region=Wolyn

xvi. http://en.wikipedia.org/wiki/Siege_of_Budapest

xvii. http://www.jewishvirtuallibrary.org/bratislava

xviii. https://en.wikipedia.org/wiki/Cinecitt%C3%A0

xix. https://www.ushmm.org/exhibition/displaced-persons/camp3b.htm

Acknowledgments

Above all—I thank G-d for protecting my father through the war, for giving him the courage to share his story, and for giving me the fortitude to fulfill my promise to him.

This memoir would not be possible without my father's willingness to stand vulnerably before me and recount his testimony. It is with immeasurable gratitude to him that this book is possible. He passed away in 2014, and I regret not having completed the work while he was still alive. Pa, I believe in my heart that you know I have kept my promise to share your story; I only hope to make you proud.

There is no stronger source of love and support than my beautiful wife, Rachel. She endured countless conversations regarding this book and stood by me throughout the process from the near beginning. Thank you, Rachel, so very much for being there every step of the way.

Equally, I thank my children. Hannah, you honor Dedushka's memory with your passionate love of Judaism; thank you so much for caring about his story and supporting me in finishing the book. Jonah, you carry my father's namesake, and are a source of love and laughter in our lives; thank you for your tenderness and affection. I also want to thank our puppy, Duke; he spent countless hours on my lap, comforting me, as I typed the pages of this memoir.

Mom, it is difficult to overstate how critical your role has been in this book. Thank you so much for supporting Pa, for making him comfortable during the recordings, and for drawing on your memory to help Pa tell his story. I can only imagine how difficult it must have been to console him after he unburdened such painful memories. I am eternally grateful for your love and support.

Growing up together with the legacy of my father's survival, my sister Sonia is the only other person who shared those childhood stories and memories with me. Thank you, Sonia, for always serving as a source of motivation and support.

My brother Lee and I spoke nearly daily about our lives, and he was always a proponent of my goal to complete this book. He too bore witness to our father's survival stories and often shared his thoughts and observations with me. Words cannot express how much I miss our conversations. Thank you so much for the love and attention you gave me.

For my nieces and nephews on my parents' side: Olivia (and your Mom, Rachel), Edan, Lev, and Eker—your Grandpa Wolf / Dedushka loved you all very much; thank you for being a source of love and joy to him and to us all.

To my dear friend: James Campagna, thank you for always being there to encourage me throughout the writing process—and in all other aspects of life. My father always held a warm place in his heart for you.

I also wish to thank my mother and father in-law Joanne and Howard Bleich, as well as my brother in-law and children, Eric, Harleigh, and Ethan Bleich for their steadfast love and support.

To my editor, Danny Wattenberg, thank you so very much for your professionalism and care.

Thank you Rabbi Craig Axler, for serving as the leader of our Jewish community, and for your kind words of support in my goal to tell my father's story. You are a *mensch* indeed.

I am honored to call Michael Kesler a friend; thank you not only for your endorsement, but for sharing your remarkable survival story in *Shards of War* and for taking the time to speak and visit with me over the years we've known one another.

Thank you, Professor Miriam Isaacs, for your endorsement of this memoir and for shining a light on the forgotten stories of the Holocaust.

All of humanity is grateful to the United States Holocaust Memorial Museum and Yad Vashem World Holocaust Remembrance Center for the dedication to preserve the memory of those lost in the Holocaust. I personally wish to thank these remarkable institutions for archiving records of my relatives and for their assistance with research for this memoir.

Last, but not least in any measure, I express sincere appreciation for my partners in this effort, Mascot Books. Thank you for the attentiveness and professionalism throughout this process.